THE
HEART
of America

THE HEART of America

Mike Trout
with Steve Halliday

ZondervanPublishingHouse
Grand Rapids, Michigan

A Division of HarperCollinsPublishers

The Heart of America
Copyright © 1998 by Mike Trout

Requests for information should be addressed to:

ZondervanPublishingHouse
Grand Rapids, Michigan 49530

Library of Congress Cataloging-in-Publication Data

Trout, Mike.
    The heart of America / Mike Trout with Steve Halliday.
        p.   cm.
    Includes bibliographical references.
    ISBN: 0-310-22008-4 (hardcover)
    1. Trout, Mike. 2. Christian biography—United States. 3. Bicycle touring—United
States. 4. United States—Description and travel. 5. United States—Religion—1960– 6.
United States—Moral conditions. I. Halliday, Steve, 1957–   .
BR1725.T68A3   1998
277.3'0829—dc21   97–47517
                                                                                                              CIP

Published in association with the literary agency of Alive Communications, Inc., 1465 Kelly
Johnson Blvd., #320, Colorado Springs, CO 80920

Interior design by Sue Vandenberg Koppenol

Printed in the United States of America

98 99 00 01 02 03 04 /❖ DC/ 10 9 8 7 6 5 4 3 2 1

Contents

CHAPTER 1

Why Are You Doing This?

The elderly man's right eyebrow arched into a question mark as we wheeled into town, our Lycra biking shorts and brightly colored shirts sharply contrasting with the gray, wrinkled contours of the old city. Even before we dismounted, we could tell it was coming. You could see it dancing on his mind. The Question. We had already heard it countless times, and before our adventure was through we'd hear it innumerable times more.

"Eh—where you fellas from?" the man asked.

"Colorado Springs," I answered.

"But you didn't ride them things from there, did ya?"

"No, you're right, we didn't. We started in Santa Monica, California, a couple of weeks ago."

"What? You're pullin' mah leg! You really came all that way—on those?"

"We really did."

"Well, I'll be. And where ya headed, then?"

"We plan to finish in a couple of weeks on a beach at the Atlantic Ocean."

"Noooooooo! Are you kiddin' me?"

"No, I'm not kidding. We're biking across the United States."

"Well, I've never seen such a thing. I got just one question for you, son." (Here it comes.)

"Yes?"

"Why?!?"

Scores of people asked us The Question in every state we visited. Why in the wide world would anyone of sound mind choose to subject himself—for five long weeks—to a 6 x 11 inch tapered perch atop a two-wheeled, leg-powered conveyance simply to travel from the West Coast of the United States to the East Coast? After giving an answer the first few times, I think I came up with the real reasons why I subjected myself to thirty-five days of discomfort, fatigue, pain, danger, and, oh yes, some incredible experiences that no one could have anticipated.

Five Key Reasons for My Trip

1. The Big Heart Scare

I gained twenty pounds shortly after Nancy and I were married in 1969, and I've been dissatisfied with my physical condition ever since. I've always been athletic and played baseball most of my life. I've enjoyed racketball, a little tennis, and most other popular sports, but as I've aged and struggled with my deteriorating abilities, my weight became a growing frustration.

I suppose my personality worked against me. I'm a Type A individual; I like to play hard and work hard. But the older I got, the more I focused on my career, and the more imbalance I created by working harder than I played. The long hours and the extended days of work cut short my exercise, and my bathroom scale showed the result.

When my family and I moved to Colorado Springs in 1991, I discovered I had high blood pressure and began taking medication to control it. I wondered how my weight had contributed to the problem. Then in June 1996 my family doctor suggested that I take a treadmill test, not because he suspected clogged arteries but because it was one of the only tests I hadn't taken. So on June 30 I visited a heart specialist. A treadmill test is an eight-minute exam in which the patient walks, then jogs on a treadmill, the slope and speed of which is increased progressively. The heart's reaction to that additional stress is recorded and the cardiologist determines whether the patient has any abnormalities. I felt fine after the test and was not out of breath, so I was surprised when the doctor said gravely, "Well, this doesn't look good."

Those are not words you like to hear upon completing a treadmill test! The doctor showed me a drop in one line that should have been flat. "I'm worried about this, Mike. I want to talk to your family doctor about it."

My heart sank (no pun intended), and I returned to my office at Focus on the Family and anxiously awaited a follow-up call. When the phone finally rang, it wasn't my doctor but one of his assistants. Now he, too, according to the assistant, was "very concerned" about my health and was advising me to have a heart catheterization. "He wants you to set that up just as soon as you possibly can," she said.

Oof! My mortality hit me like a ton of bricks. All kinds of things started going through my mind. What if I didn't make it through the surgery? Even though the procedure is described as common and simple and fairly minor, I knew all surgery entails some risk. I struggled with telling anyone, even my own family. So I kept silent.

That July 4 was one of the most emotionally draining holidays I've ever experienced. The importance of everything seemed exaggerated. My interactions with family and friends were dearer to me than they had ever been. I've always enjoyed fireworks, but the ones I saw that Independence Day were the most remarkable I'd ever witnessed. I couldn't help thinking, *Perhaps this will be the last time we'll be together like this.* Isn't it funny the way the mind can distort things? But that's what I was thinking.

Finally, the day before I was to enter the hospital (several days had passed, but it took me that long to work through my emotions), I pulled myself together and told Nancy I was about to undergo a heart catheterization. Understandably, she was angry that I hadn't told her sooner. She made it clear she needed to be brought in on such important decisions immediately. Then her anger quickly changed to deep concern, and we started to call loved ones to let them know I was facing surgery that could uncover a serious medical problem. What a blessing we have as believers to be lifted up by the prayers of family and friends. And what peace I began to enjoy as I awaited my visit to the hospital.

I was a bit surprised to discover that the patient is awake throughout the entire process. The doctor makes a small incision close to the groin, inserts a fiber optic probe into a large artery there, and snakes the probe up to the heart. Then a dye is injected right into the arteries of the heart and everyone in attendance watches as that dye spreads out. The dye shows if any arteries are clogged and, if so, to what degree. An X-ray device had been placed above my chest and a monitor, like a TV screen, was located over my head, so I could see everything the doctor and nurses saw.

When we reached this point, the doctor said, "There's no problem here. We must have had a false reading on the treadmill test. That does occur occasionally. I thought I would probably see you within the next twelve months for some bypass surgery, but now I don't believe we'll get together again professionally for at least thirty years."

I can't begin to express how relieved I was at that moment—but it was relief tinged with anger. That false reading had created a tremendous amount of anxiety in my life, even if it had been for only a few days! But the news was good. I spent the rest of the afternoon recovering in the hospital, went home that evening, and life went on.

It was a follow-up visit to the cardiologist that prompted my decision to take the bike trip. The doctor explained again that while his findings were positive, I did have an imbalance between my HDL (High-Density Lipoprotein, the good cholesterol) and the LDL (Low-Density Lipoprotein, the bad cholesterol). My bad cholesterol numbers were fine, but my level of good cholesterol was low. He said there were a number of ways to raise it, including some medications, but the best and recommended way of raising my HDL count was a vigorous exercise program.

That was the impetus I needed. It pushed me over the edge and forced me to change my lifestyle. Within days I was seriously considering a cross-country bike trip I had only talked and dreamed about before. Soon after that Fourth of July in 1996 I became determined to bike from sea to shining sea.

2. A Baby Boomer Turns Fifty

The first Baby Boomers (those born from 1946 to 1964) started turning fifty in 1996; my turn was slated for the following year. Before my big day I started noticing the vast attention being showered on us half-centenarians. Author Bob Greene, for example, published a book with the not-so-celebratory title, *The 50-Year Dash: The Feelings, Foibles, and Fears of Being Half a Century Old*. It was a sobering thought, this turning fifty, but one I learned to contemplate with satisfaction and even a little glee.

I confess I enjoyed reading an interview with humorist Dave Barry written by nationally syndicated columnist Jeffrey Zaslow.[1] Barry turned fifty in 1997 and said he viewed himself "as an aging boomer who is losing his grip on what's hip." He had just published his eighteenth book, *Dave Barry's Book of Bad Songs,* and was struck by the fact that what used to be cool isn't anymore. "Just look at my old role models, Exhibit A being Burt Reynolds," Barry said. "He used to be so cool." No longer; nowadays only a fifty-year-old would think of linking the terms "Burt Reynolds" and "cool." But Zaslow did have some counsel. "If, like Barry, you're hopelessly rooted in the culture and music of your youth," he wrote, "he has advice. 'Ask yourself: Are songs getting worse or am I getting older? The answer: Songs are getting worse, and you're getting older. You have to accept that you are getting uncooler by the second.'"

Tough news for a guy like me . . . or for any guy over forty. Sometimes I just can't believe that I'm not still in my twenties. I know this sounds trite, but it really does seem like it was just a few days ago when I made the baseball team. I used to think that fifty was ancient, but here I was, approaching my fiftieth birthday. Was there anything I could do to recover some of my youthful vigor—maybe even a little coolness? That's when the idea of riding a bicycle across America became a serious consideration. What better adventure could there be for an aging Baby Boomer who wants to prove he isn't quite over the hill just yet. Others might have their mid-life crisis descend on them; I would schedule mine, and it would be awesome!

3. If He Could Do It, So Can I

One of my biggest inspirations for taking the bike trip came from my uncle, Tom Gilfoy. Tom took up bicycling a number of years ago after he underwent heart bypass surgery, and in 1995 took forty-four days to pedal from Santa Monica, California, to Myrtle Beach, South Carolina. I was fascinated by his stories of the places he visited and the people he met on his solo, cross-continental adventure.

By the way, Tom didn't take his trip until after he had celebrated his sixty-second birthday. So if he could bike by himself from ocean to ocean at the mature age of sixty-two, why shouldn't I, with a dozen fewer years under my belt, be able to do the same thing?

4. I Remember Years Ago . . .

As I approached my fiftieth birthday, I began to realize that more and more of my conversation concerned events that had taken place years, even decades, before. I'd talk about my early career in radio or a certain group I sang with in college or a trip we took dozens of years before. Seldom did I find myself describing some new venture or enterprise. And I began asking, Why is that? The discovery was disquieting. I was in a rut.

I finally decided that a bicycle trip across the country would get me out of that rut. If nothing else, it would give me plenty of new things to talk about. After all, who really wants to hear about a throw out at home plate from center field in a softball game two decades ago?

I don't want to be too critical of my fellow Boomers, but as I look around it seems as if we could all use a little motivation to try something new. Think about your own life. When was the last time you did something quite out of the ordinary? How has your weekly routine varied in the last five or six years? We had become comfortable living in the past, and when that happens, we miss out on so many of the riches that God has created for our enjoyment. One of the main reasons I decided to go ahead with my dream to bike across America was to prove to myself (and others) that we Boomers are still up for some adventure.

5. *Has the Faith of This Nation Flatlined?*

For more than twelve years, I have been the radio cohost for Focus on the Family, a wonderful organization devoted to helping American families. During that time, I've helped interview hundreds of top communicators. Some feel the country is in good shape; others lament the loss of family values. Some say spirituality is on the rise; others insist that God's blessing on America is a distant memory. I've heard the opinions of scores of leaders—from influential politicians and best-selling authors to the clergy of our biggest churches. I've talked with those who survey the masses and write the commentaries that help shape our culture. Like many of you, I care deeply about our country and the condition of the American family. But what is it really like out there where moms and dads are trying to raise their children?

What better way to find out than to ride a bike through the small towns and the big cities of this diverse land of ours. I could find out what ordinary Americans think and care about. I could get beyond the headlines, the sound bites, the blur of surveys, and listen to regular people. I decided I wanted to put my ear to the ground where many live: communities with names like Daggett, Great Bend, Tribune, Pagosa Springs, and Harriman. By doing so I hoped that I could find the still-beating heart of a great country.

Getting Ready

Once I decided to plunge ahead with the trip, it quickly became clear I had a lot of work to do. You can't simply hop on a bike and pedal across a 3000-mile expanse—filled with mountains and plains and valleys and rivers and angry dogs—without first preparing for your journey. (At least not if you want to finish what you start.) My own preparation focused on four key areas.

1. *Physical*

I weighed 167 pounds when I began to prepare myself for the trip. Immediately I made several basic changes in my eating habits. I reduced my fat intake dramatically—I tried to drop below ten grams a day—which enabled me to trim my weight as quickly as possible. I reduced my sugar intake. To get my metabolism going first thing in the morning, I tried to eat a well-balanced breakfast within a half hour of rising. I made lunch my big meal of the day and never ate dinner after 7:00 P.M. When I did eat at night, the meal was always small. I watched my diet religiously and didn't cheat one single time.

I also embarked on a vigorous exercise regimen. For some time my family has enjoyed a membership at a local athletic club, but I had been an infrequent visitor. I became a regular. Every day I rode a stationary bike at the highest level I could manage for as long as I could stand in order to get my heart rate up. After riding the bike, I would lift weights, doing upper body exercises one day and lower body workouts the next. Because the leg muscles are especially important for bicycling, they received the majority of my attention. Leg presses are excellent for the hamstrings, quads, and calves. I also did (and continue to do) at least 200 sit-ups every night, working various muscle groups of the abdomen. The stomach muscles are at the center of everything, and I didn't dare neglect them.

My target was my newlywed weight at just under 150 pounds. It took dogged perseverance, commitment, and sacrifice, but it paid off. Within thirty days, I started to see some dramatic results. When I left on the trip May 10, I had dropped to 147 pounds (and lost another 5 pounds on the ride). Carrying no extra weight is a blessing as you travel!

I know some might say, "Well, Mike, that's a little too harsh, don't you think? A little too severe. That's just too quick." I don't agree. Any less of a commitment creates an environment where cheating is almost inevitable. Too often people start the process of weight loss and play with it, toy with it, make only a little change here, a little change there. They don't realize how easy it is to swerve off the desired path and undermine everything they're trying to accomplish.

In February 1997 the bike I would use on my adventure arrived and I began riding as often as weather would permit. Of course, Colorado in February, March, and April provides fewer of those days than I would have liked! Some days, the cold was unbearable. I would start out from the house, bundled up with thick gloves, heavy jacket, and long pants, and get only half a mile from home before I'd turn around and head back. When the mercury dipped below thirty, I found it too uncomfortable to ride. Still, I knew I needed "saddle time" to prepare my backside for the long trek across the United States. Before my adventure began, I rode either the road bike or the stationary bike every day, getting in at least 150 miles every week.

I began telling everybody I knew about the trip. I wanted to force myself into a box from which I could not easily escape. And there were doubters! A few who heard of my plans openly questioned my ability and determination to see them through. But they only made me all the more determined to accomplish my goal.

2. Equipment and Supplies

A bike is a pretty simple piece of equipment. It has two wheels with tires that need air and with spokes that must remain tightened so the wheel doesn't get out of round. It has a bottom bracket, a top bracket, bearings, pedals, a frame, handle bars, a seat, brakes, chain rings in the front, gears in the back, a chain connecting them all, and deraillers to facilitate shifting. All these moving parts need occasional adjustment.

Once you've learned a few basics, anyone can take care of a bike. It's like most things: If you keep track of it, if you listen to it, if you watch it and keep it clean, the likelihood of a breakdown is pretty rare—especially if you've purchased a quality piece of equipment.

Enter Tom Ritchey.

I met Tom in the mid- to late '80s. Tom is one of the premier bicycle manufacturers in the country and a longtime supporter of Focus on the Family. We had spent a few days together at a Focus on the Family outing at Elk Canyon Ranch in Montana.

Once I decided on the bike trip, I called Tom, told him of my plans, and placed an order for a sixteen-speed Road Logic road bike. Tom uses a steel alloy frame (rather than aluminum, carbon fiber, or titanium), believing that it gives a more comfortable ride due to greater flexibility. His bikes are professional quality, proven over years of difficult racing.

Tom took it upon himself to pull together the rest of the equipment I would need. Every week or so, I'd receive "care packages" from him stuffed with clothing, shoes, a helmet, gloves, tools—everything he thought I should take for a safe trip across the country. And if he didn't send it, he would tell me about it—extra tubes, spare tires, a chain cleaner, WD-40, whatever might be required to take care of mishaps.

Eventually we opted for Presta valves on the tires (they're smaller and hold air better than the usual variety) and cleated biking shoes that clip into small, triangular pedals. When the trip began, the gear included fifteen extra tubes, six spare tires, a tube-patching and tire-changing kit, a pump, a maintenance stand (made by Ultimate), miscellaneous tools, chain oil, a chain-cleaning unit, and a dozen or so rags.

But Tom was not content. He kept asking me, "Have you thought about having a support van, a sag wagon, to go along with you?" No, I hadn't. At first I didn't think I wanted one. But the more I discussed the ride with others and the more times that question was asked, the more I thought, Hmmm, perhaps that might not be too bad of an idea after all. Eventually I rented a large Dodge van from a local car dealer at the unbelievable price of two-hundred dollars for the entire five-week trip. Thank you, Perkins Motor City Dodge! Even with that good price, it was more expensive to rent the van, pay for its gas, and cover meal and motel expenses for a van driver than it was for me to make the trip solo, but the increase in comfort and security was well worth it.

Just as important as the bike equipment was the clothing. Here's what I did on that score:

1 pair of quality cycling shoes with cleats that match the
    pedals
5 pairs of thin biking socks
4 pairs of short, padded cycling pants
1 pair of long cycling pants for cold weather
1 lightweight, waterproof, cycling jacket
1 warm cycling jacket
1 pair of fingerless gloves
1 pair of warm cycling gloves

1 well-fitting helmet

1 pair of quality sunglasses with interchangeable lenses
   for various light conditions

Of course, on any long trip you have to get intimately familiar with laundromats along the way. You might be able to leave home without certain credit cards, but not without laundry soap. Washing shorts, shirts, and socks after each wearing is a necessity. Otherwise . . .

And how about other supplies? My oldest daughter, Rebekah, who is one half of a morning team on a hot adult contemporary secular radio station in Colorado Springs, was very helpful in that area. Her station exchanged spot advertisements for needed equipment—$1,000 worth of equipment from Bicycle Village, to be exact. In addition, a local company donated a box of one hundred energy bars (called "Peak Bars") at the start of the trip and sent another box at the halfway point. We received several hundred bottles of Power Aide and Ocean Spray drinks through other contacted trades, while Focus on the Family paid for our two cell phones in return for several on-the-road updates and hundreds of radio station interviews.

3. Personnel

Initially I had planned to follow my uncle's example and take the trip solo; there's a certain level of challenge in that. But right from the start, my son-in-law Brian Slivka began asking about the possibility of joining me.

I had known Brian for several years before he married my middle daughter, Amy, and I knew he was an experienced bike rider. The thought of having a second person on the trip—someone to talk with, to help with any breakdowns, to assist in any difficult or unsafe situations—appealed to me. I also looked forward to getting to know him better. So I said, "If you can work it out, then I'll be happy to have you come along."

He did work it out, and Brian made the most of his trip by arranging with Rebekah's radio station, Magic FM, to do daily reports from the road. In turn, the station invited listeners to pledge money in support of a camp for inner city youth called Kids Across America, a ministry Brian loves. Every morning Brian was to call in with a joke (later in the book you can decide whether any of them are funny) and a trip progress report. The station gave him special T-shirts to hand out along the way, and its unflagging enthusiasm for our efforts kept us all encouraged.

But I wasn't through putting together my "team." If you have a van, you also need a van driver. For that I recruited my father-in-law, Ted Kildal, who graciously gave up five weeks of his time to ferry our supplies and equipment from one coast to the other. At the end of the trip, he and his wife, Charlotte, even drove the van back to Colorado Springs while Brian and I flew back in pressurized comfort.

The last member of the team joined us the night before we pedaled away from the Santa Monica pier. Steve Halliday would take pictures, serve as "trip secretary," and help me write this book.

4. Route

It's one thing to decide to bike across the nation from the Pacific to the Atlantic; it's another to design a workable route. Fortunately, much of my work on this point already had been done by my uncle on his cross-country bike trip in 1995. I decided to follow his basic course. I, too, planned to start out in Santa Monica and end in Myrtle Beach.

For the most part, we followed his route. Although we didn't end up in Myrtle Beach as he did—that's a story for later—we did ramble over many of the same roads he had used two years earlier. It was fun to compare our experiences with his journal as we passed through many of the same towns he had visited on his solo trek across the country. And yet our trip would be uniquely our own, with its own set of highlights and drudgeries.

Finally, with training completed, equipment and supplies gathered, route chosen, and team members secured, there was only one thing left to do: Hit the road!

And they're off . . . almost!

A few days before our planned departure on May 10, 1997, Brian and Amy drove the fully supplied van from Colorado Springs to La Cañada, California, where we would stay for two nights at my uncle Tom's home. He and his wife Dody were on an adventure of their own to Africa, but had given us enthusiastic permission to use their house as a jumping-off station for our cross-country journey.

Friday night, May 9, I stretched out on a bed and tried to sleep. I tried to not think about the journey that would soon begin, but couldn't put it out of my mind. Would I make it? Would injuries slow me down? Do I really have what it takes? What will I find when I pedal into the hundreds of towns and cities along the way?

Finally, I did drift off to sleep and dreamed about the adventure that lay ahead.

CHAPTER 2

Just 3,149 Miles to Go

It was time. May 10.

After all the hubbub of the last few months, the morning of my bicycling odyssey had finally arrived. The training rides were over; now it was time for the real thing. The May 1997 edition of *Focus on the Family* magazine already was in homes across the country, and there on page fourteen was a green three-inch map of the United States bisected by a red line—my planned route—stretching from California to South Carolina. An accompanying article, headlined "Mike Trout to Bike Across America," told readers that

> Mike Trout could be biking into a town near you! Yes, the longtime co-host of the "Focus on the Family" broadcast is embarking on a quest to ride his 21-speed Tom Ritchey bike on the old Route 66 during May and early June. He will start on the beach in Santa Monica, Calif., and pedal to the Atlantic Ocean in South Carolina. His 3,000-mile transcontinental journey will take him through many small towns and cities, and he hopes to say hello to "Focus on the Family" listeners along the way.

Kind of hard to back out with *that* kind of publicity.

Brian and I headed out the door, running mostly on adrenaline. I hadn't slept well for several nights and that last night before we left, I hadn't gotten more than four or five hours of sleep. As we headed for the van and the drive to Santa Monica, all I could think of was pushing off. I had no great, swelling words of inspiration. No predictions. No speeches. No deep profundities. I remember once hearing a football coach being interviewed before a big game with an arch rival. The reporter asked the coach what he had told his team before they left the locker room and headed out onto the battlefield. "I just told them to do their best," the coach said. "At this point, you're either ready or you're not, and no pep talk is going to make all that much difference."

It was time to do our best.

Mind Games

We arrived on the Santa Monica pier shortly after 11:00 A.M. When you ride a bike from coast to coast, there's a little tradition you follow to symbolize that you went the *entire* distance. When you leave, you start with your back tire in the ocean. And when you arrive, you dip your front tire into the ocean on the other side of the continent. As we got to the beach, two freelance video professionals hired by Channel 38 of Chicago were waiting to record our departure. The camera started to roll as our rear wheels entered the ocean and continued filming as we pedaled past the colorful stands and shops and visitors crowding the Santa Monica pier. Finally, a little before noon, we were under way. It felt great!

I couldn't help but think "big thoughts" as we left the pier under sunny skies, with the temperature a balmy seventy degrees. It was somewhat sobering to think of all the people who had helped make this adventure possible. As a result of publicity from Focus on the Family, I knew that literally thousands of people around the country were praying for my safety. How often we forget what it means to be part of God's great family, but in this moment, with more than three thousand miles of uncertainty ahead of me, it was reassuring to know that I wasn't alone.

As I pushed into the slight headwind, my mind drifted to an event that occurred almost three decades before on a beach only a few miles down the coast. There, on that shore, a remarkable movement of God began and continues to this day, still thrilling believers and confounding skeptics. On a single day in 1971, more than 900 young people—mostly members of California's radical hippie culture, the "flower children" of the late '60s—declared their enthusiastic allegiance to Jesus Christ and were baptized in the Pacific Ocean. The man who was the head of that joyous celebration was Chuck Smith, pastor of a new little church in Costa Mesa, called Calvary Chapel.

For two years in the mid-1970s, Calvary Chapel Costa Mesa helped lead more than 20,000 people to faith in Christ and registered more than 8,000 baptisms. The church's growth rate that decade was calculated at nearly 10,000 percent. For several years, whenever it secured or built new facilities to handle the mushrooming crowds, it found on "opening day" that its new buildings were already packed to overflowing. Today Calvary Chapel Costa Mesa estimates (there is no "official" member-ship) that about 25,000 people attend services each week, with over 650 congregations nationwide (and an additional 134 internationally) affiliated with Calvary Chapel.

Pretty good for a church that started out in 1965 with twenty-five worshipers and whole rooms full of discouragement!

Many of the changes we've seen in worship today had their genesis in Costa Mesa. A more casual atmosphere, with an acceptance of the person, not the style of clothing, began in those early services. The praise choruses, which millions now sing every Sunday, were first lifted heavenward from that Southern California outpost.

You might think it odd of me to reminisce about this church while starting to pedal across America, but sometimes big challenges turn us toward those things that are most impor-tant to us. I was part of the music business during the early and mid-'70s and watched with wonder the metamorphosis that took place within Christian music. Around the world, people imitated these artists who were given a platform for their con-temporary style of worship. It was Calvary Chapel that gave this breath of fresh air to the world. In fact, Calvary Chapel has a long history of giving.

And there's a personal link. In 1993, as my then future son-in-law Brian went forward at a Promise Keepers Conference to dramatically dedicate his life to Christ, it was a group birthed at Calvary Chapel, the Maranatha Singers, who provided the musical background for his commitment. If you are the mom or dad of a young woman, you know how much we long to see our kids find partners who share our faith in Christ. Now here I am, pedaling, trying to keep up with my daughter's young husband, and I want to shout a big word of praise to God for the way he blessed Chuck Smith and the good people at Calvary Chapel.

I'm sure there are times in your own church when you wonder if all the effort is worth it. Let's face it. Church is tough business. Getting people together to worship and serve the community, finding enough volunteers to teach or to change diapers in the nursery, and working through the nitty-gritty and the endless debates about music and building programs that divide people can get discouraging at times. As I watched Brian grinding out the miles on his own special mission to help people, I was so thankful that God gave us his church.

A patch of gravel quickly brings my soaring soul back to reality. Hey, only 3,149 miles to go!

Leaving This Town

From the pier, we rode north on Ocean and then east on Santa Monica Boulevard. Our trip almost came to a screeching halt when Brian hit a pothole and nearly toppled over. Remarkably, it would be the closest we'd come on the entire journey to taking a fall.

On our way out of town we rode on Sepulveda Boulevard, named after Francisco Sepulveda, a rancher and soldier who lived in the area during the late eighteenth and early nineteenth centuries. Long before being named a boulevard in 1930, the road was an important trail linking vital points along the San Fernando Valley. I obtained my first driver's license in Glendale, California, on my birthday in 1963, and since then have driven sections of Old Sepulveda Boulevard scores of times. But on this day I would see it as never before.

We soon passed the Los Angeles National Cemetery, a permanent resting place for over 80,000 residents dating back to 1889. Scores of giant Eucalyptus and purple blooming jacaranda trees stand guard against the bustling life all around the 114-acre perimeter.

On the road we were joined by dozens of other cyclists, most of them going the other way. Everywhere we looked, it seemed, we saw spandex shorts, bike helmets of all conceivable hues, and bikers both shirted and shirtless. The campus of the University of California in Los Angeles, better known as UCLA, is less than a mile away and most of the riders had the unmistakable look of vibrant youth. I was glad I wouldn't have to follow a whole group of them for the next thirty days.

We passed twelve-foot-high, manicured hedges shaped like refrigerators on our left, and the Santa Monica mountains on both sides. Graffiti scarred the highway dividers and let us know, officially, that we were still in Los Angeles.

At the top of Sepulcher Pass we flew through a tunnel at thirty miles per hour and thought it felt good to get out of the heat, if only for a few seconds. On our right, bottle brush, date palms, and red Oleander blossoms decorated the roadside. A panhandler with a twisted right leg and sporting a blonde, scraggly beard, held a hand-scrawled cardboard sign in front of his blue T-shirt: "I am sorry for this! Things will get better for all of us, you will see. God bless."

By the time we dropped into the valley, the temperature was well into the nineties. It was because of just such scorching heat during the summer months that my grandfather and his two boys (the oldest being my dad) in the early '30s dug by hand one of the first in-ground swimming pools in the area. In the foothills of Burbank (above "beautiful downtown") at the east edge of the San Fernando Valley, they created a backyard oasis. Here my earliest memories were created, mental snapshots of family gatherings at the little white house on Palm Avenue. More than thirty aunts, uncles, cousins, and in-laws often enjoyed the shade of a large sycamore, barbecuing hamburgers and plunging into the cool, clear pool. I can still see my grandfather standing in his bathing suit, ready to perform a flawless dive into the deep end while the rest of us scattered to the edges. Probably more than a hundred men and women, boys and girls, have learned to swim in that pool—and the number is still growing! What a marvelous investment in the lives of so many was made through the efforts of just a few.

My grandmother still lives in that house. She's ninety-three. (My grandfather died in 1988.) She's great to visit because she helps me remember that little has changed on that hillside lot. The front porch swing still creaks, the sycamore drops its leaves about the same time each year, the rough cement bottom of the pool will still rub your feet raw if you swim all day . . . and if you close your eyes you just might hear again the voices of family members who have "gone home." Everyone should have a place where time stands still! Those were wonderful, warm days, and on this Saturday, as I pedaled familiar territory, I could have used a refreshing dip in the old pool.

Halfway across the valley floor we crossed Sherman Way. At that intersection we are only a few blocks from one of the country's megachurches. This one was begun by a youth pastor named Jack Hayford who called his congregation "Church on the Way"—Sherman Way, that is. I can't think of Jack Hayford without remembering one of the more important experiences in the life of Dr. James Dobson, my boss and the president of Focus on the Family. In 1990 Dr. Dobson suffered a mild heart attack and was recovering in a San Gabriel Valley hospital. An intense loneliness settled on him and he prayed that God would send someone to help ease his strong feelings of isolation. A full ten days before he uttered this prayer God had, again and again, put Dr. Dobson on the mind and heart of Pastor Hayford, who at the time was leaving for Japan. Upon his return to the States, Pastor Hayford felt divinely constrained to visit the hospital. He later told Dr. Dobson, "I wondered how I could presume to do that when there were so many people who loved and surrounded you." Nevertheless, he did stop by the hospital room and said, "The Lord has spoken to my heart that you are lonely."

Dr. Dobson could hardly believe his ears. Later, in recalling that visit, he said, "God knows what we need before we ask, but I've never seen him answer prayer that way before. The Lord quoted me word-for-word to Jack *ten days before I prayed that prayer!*"

Mission Statement

Given the ubiquitous development today, with pavement everywhere, it's difficult to envision the rural beauty of the San Fernando Valley when it was awash in orange trees and dotted with farmhouses. Yet that's what it looked like less than two generations ago. After World War II, thousands of parents of Baby Boomers flocked to the valley and bought up the fast-growing, inexpensive homes that replaced the fragrant orange groves. By the early '60s, only a few small farms remained in defiance of "progress."

One institution which still remains is the Old Mission San Fernando Rey de España, established on September 8, 1797. It's a good "photo op" and as soon as we reached it, we pulled over. This was the seventeenth mission to be constructed in an inland chain connecting San Gabriel with the missions located around San Francisco Bay. Across the street, Brand Park is planted with flowers and shrubs from all twenty-one missions in the chain. This rebuilt, 243-foot-long hospice is still the largest adobe building in California. Today it houses demonstration rooms that depict old mission activities, including cattle hide processing, for which the mission was famous. By 1818 the mission had assembled a herd of 21,000 cattle, using them for rawhide (in those days iron spikes were scarce and rawhide was used in all types of construction to hold buildings together).

The notion of a mission in the United States seems archaic to most of us, but in California it was an outpost from which dedicated followers of God attempted to spread the Christian faith. I think it's more than symbolic that one of this mission's activities was producing material that held things together. That's not a bad mission for today's church—to be the folks in our communities who hold things together rather than cause divisions.

The First Setback

By mid-afternoon on a cloudless, sizzling day, we stopped for a brief rest at the entrance to Sunshine Canyon Landfill of Browning Ferris Industries of California. Not exactly the best place for a little nutrition break, but Brian and I both gulped down another Power Aide and greedily munched on Peak Bars. Now I'm no Michael Jordan (which is why these good companies did not sign me up to a mega-million-dollar contract to endorse their products), but they did give us a lot of free stuff, so they at least deserve a little commercial here: "Tired of gagging on expensive energy bars that taste like construction adhesive? Try a PEAK BAR. I think you'll taste and feel what thousands have—superior flavor, a satisfying experience, and oodles of energy."

Too bad I couldn't strike a similar deal with a good sun-block maker. Despite copious amounts of SPF 15 slathered on every square inch of unprotected skin, we already noticed scarlet patches scorched by the blistering sun—the back of our necks and the tops of our ears now radiated their own heat. No need for panic, but this was just the first day and we were still a long way from crossing our first state border.

Too soon our break was over. We put on headbands to keep perspiration from stinging our eyes. We never sweated like this in Colorado during our training; it was either too cold or too dry. I now recalled those days in late winter when I would be dressed in a long-sleeved shirt, long pants, a riding jacket, full-fingered gloves, and an extra riding cap under my helmet. The temperature hovered in the thirties and it would take at least a half hour for me to warm up. During those rides I dreamed of warm summer days, short-sleeved jerseys, thin socks, and a gentle breeze at my back. I now remembered those winter training trips as cool, not cold, and I wished for a little snow on the side of the road. How fickle we become when faced with extremes!

Once more we snapped on our helmets and mounted our bicycles to attack the next leg of our long journey. A few minutes into our climb we ran into road construction and a sign that confused us. The sign read, "The Old Road," and pointed in an unexpected direction. Which way were we supposed to go? Our map was of no help—the AAA state maps we used throughout our trip were great for macro-planning but nearly useless for deciding whether this or that county road led to bliss or . . . something else entirely. We briefly debated our options and made our decision.

As we painfully ground our way up the mountain, it quickly became clear that this was our toughest climb yet—under the most unforgiving sun. Within moments the sweat began pouring down our foreheads and surging over saturated headbands, salty drops stinging our eyes and obscuring our vision. Our legs, not yet fully agreeing with pedaling across a continent, screamed that the task was simply too much. We ignored their pleas and pedaled on. I sent the van ahead to scout out our next turn.

About half an hour later the van returned ... bearing dismal news. *We had taken the wrong route!* Our van drivers Ted and Steve knew something was amiss when they passed a sign saying, "Welcome to Santa Clarita." They asked patrons in a Carrows restaurant for directions and discovered we had misread our signs. From the other direction, Old Sierra Highway is clearly marked to Soledad Canyon Road. From the direction we had come, it was not.

We had just grunted up five miles of a monster hill, miles our tires were never meant to touch! Not only had we expended precious energy we could ill afford to waste, but we had gone five miles out of our way—a minor inconvenience for drivers zipping by at sixty air-conditioned miles per hour, but a disaster for cyclists inching up a hill at seven mph.

Licking our wounds, we tucked the bikes into the van and headed into town to eat. I groused about our error as we settled into Carrows, where we ordered a late lunch before heading back down the mountain to find the correct route. Already the evidence of my sleep deprivation was beginning to show; I was starting to lose control of my emotions. I couldn't believe it and was frustrated at the way I was letting this first mistake get to me. Researchers say that at least 50 percent of the U.S. population suffer from some form of sleeping difficulty, which might explain why some people seem to be angry so much of the time. Many say sleep disorders are related to our fast-paced lifestyle and lack of physical exertion. For good reason the book of Ecclesiastes says, "The sleep of a laboring man is sweet" (5:12 KJV).

What's Happening Inside?

By the time we returned to our missed junction, our watches read nearly 5:00 P.M. It wasn't easy to restart our engines—whenever I start biking, I feel a little like a train, barely moving at first, then lurching, then moving steadily, and finally hitting my riding pace—but soon we were once again making progress. We noticed numerous white crosses dotting the sides of the road, marking fatal crashes. One cross, decorated with a wreath, memorialized a man who would be missed in three crucial roles:

	F	
Son	a	Husband
	t	
	h	
	e	
	r	

How profoundly sad that in one devastating moment, the lives of parents, spouse, and children were changed forever! Two of those roles you choose and, with them, you accept the responsibilities. Being a son is the result of someone else's choice, but that, too, carries just as great a responsibility.

My mother was diagnosed with cancer six years ago. When the reality of her condition hit me, I began to seriously think about my headship in the family. Since then I have spent more time than ever with both of my parents. I call them regularly and talk with them much more frequently than I used to. They're not going to be here forever and there will come a point when they'll both be gone and I'll be the male figurehead of the family. I remember talking with Dr. Dobson about this when his mom died and he realized he was the only one of his family left. I am the last Trout in our line. As the only son in my family, I was the only one to carry the Trout name forward. I have three daughters who each will carry forward another man's name. When my parents are gone, my role as a son disappears. When I am gone, our Trout family name disappears.

As I rode by the "Son, Husband, Father" cross on the side of the road, a story from Guy Doud drifted through my mind. When Guy, who now is a well-known author and speaker, was heading off to college, his parents gave him a pack of note cards with self-addressed, stamped envelopes. "Please write," his mother said to him. "It would mean so much to hear from you." Guy said he rushed away with a promise to send at least one card every week. Years later, after his folks had both died and college was a distant memory, Guy was unpacking a long-forgotten box and found the cards, unused, still ready to wing home a message of love to a waiting mom and dad.

If you are blessed to still have one or both of your parents, have you talked with them lately?

Before I know it, my role as father will also change dramatically. Two of my three daughters are married and out of our home, and our last daughter will likely leave the nest in the next year. Within a window of just a few years, some pretty dramatic changes will be taking place in my life. Hey, put a middle-aged guy on a bike, run him up and down the wrong mountain, and he starts getting philosophical. And all the crosses along the road sure make you think about these things. Who am I? What kind of final patriarch will I be for the Trout family? How will I be remembered when I'm gone? I suppose if I learn nothing else on this trip, it will still be worthwhile if I answer these questions. Maybe you can answer them for yourself.

On our next hill I suffered our first flat (mark it for posterity at 5:25 P.M.). It took only seven minutes to change, and then we were off again. I was glad Marlen Wells wasn't there to remind me of one of my early attempts at repairing a puncture. Marlen is a Canadian friend who's attending Denver Seminary. He's been a part of the professional side of bicycling for many years. He and his wife, Marilyn, run a ministry out of their home called the International Christian Cycling Club. Months before, during one of my training rides, I had attempted to patch a hole in my rear tire only to find out five minutes later—when it quickly deflated—that I had placed the glue and patch just to the side of the problem. I've regretted telling Marlen about that embarrassing mistake ever since.

By 6:10 P.M. we had traveled forty-seven miles and decided to call it a night. Not too bad for starting at nearly noon! But we would have to do much better in the days ahead. We packed the bikes in the van and headed back to my uncle's home in La Cañada, hoping that our second day would be free of unplanned detours.

Trying to Join the Century Club

The next day—our first full day of riding—the overriding question in my mind was: Could we make the 100-plus-mile average I'd scheduled? During the preparation process, there had been doubters. Months before, at a friend's home in

Colorado Springs, we enjoyed an evening meal and warm conversation with a number of couples. Snow still blanketed the ground and any kind of exercise was painful to contemplate in the freezing temperatures. After dinner questions about the upcoming bike trip were fired my way. One man in particular wondered if Brian and I had ridden 100 miles yet, and I had to admit we had not. From that moment on, every time I saw this doubter he would ask again, "Have you ridden 100 miles yet?" His pessimism locked a shackle around my ankle that I wouldn't unlock until this second day of the trip. If preparation paves the road to success, then negative comments are the speed bumps!

As we rode off on our bikes, an unwelcome sign announced, "Gusty wind area next fifty-one miles." This wasn't going to be easy! Learning to climb hills efficiently is a key part of any serious bicyclist's training. You look for those places where you can push until your lungs feel like they're swelling to the handlebars. Those who live in flat areas go out on gusty days and pedal into the wind to simulate a steep incline. Perhaps today the gusts would be at our backs.

We climbed nearly all morning, the wind in our faces the whole time. So much for the hope of a gentle breeze pushing us along.

Other than a tailwind, the wind is a mortal enemy of any bicyclist. I'd much rather pedal uphill with no wind than pedal on flat ground with wind. A hill always crests and offers a nice descent on the other side; but wind can unrelentingly oppose you for hours, even days. Whenever the hills loomed steep and the wind blew stiff, I thought of James's admonition that great growth comes through adversity. *But Lord,* I thought, *must I grow this strong . . . today?* To quote Gollum from Tolkien's *Lord of the Rings,* "It's nasssssty and we don't likes it."

Today was Mother's Day, and we celebrated in a little restaurant in Acton, California.

"We're sorry you have to work on Mother's Day," I told our waitress.

"Honey, don't worry about it," she replied. "I celebrated it yesterday. Besides, I've worked on Mother's Day for the past several years. I'm used to it."

Well, I don't think I'd be. Earlier I had called my mother to wish her a happy Mother's Day. She is a very special lady. I dedicated my first book to her like this: "This book is dedicated to the bravest person I know. At age seventeen she met and married a young naval officer from California and then within days was on a train traveling 3,000 miles away from her home in Virginia to live with her husband's parents. There she patiently waited for his return from the Pacific in World War II. Today, at age sixty-seven, this Southern lady has just celebrated fifty years of holy matrimony to the same old guy from the West Coast. In between she did a million things right, including raising three children, two sweet girls and one strong-willed son. The last four years she has courageously battled cancer, again patiently and prayerfully waiting." Mom is still a marvel, and I didn't want a little bike trip to keep me from wishing her a happy Mother's Day.

I also called Nancy for the same reason. Already I missed her. I don't do a good enough job of telling her that, and I promised myself I would attempt to improve. When she's not around, I miss her wisdom and insight. I use her as a resource for valuable input; she sees things and understands things that I just don't. When we sit down to talk and I describe experiences or concerns from work, I'm often probing her reaction because I know her mind works differently than does mine. She's much more impulsive and oftentimes much more emotional in her responses; I'm more reasoned and usually less impassioned. I value her perspective immensely. It would have been wonderful to have her on the bike trip because she would have seen things in people and events that I just don't pick up on. She would have helped me understand in a different way what we were seeing and experiencing. I missed her.

Later that day we'd also be missing my daughter Amy. She had accompanied us in the van for the first two days of our adventure, and Ted and Steve were set to take her to Van Nuys to catch a shuttle to Los Angeles International Airport, where she'd hop a flight back to Colorado Springs. I remember thinking, *No doubt the phone bills from their house will go up, starting tonight.* Brian and Amy had been married only a year and a half at the time of our trip, and honeymoon was still in their eyes.

They met when they were in college at the University of Colorado in Colorado Springs; they had at least one class together. Brian was almost painfully shy. Amy knew he was interested in her, and yet it took him literally months to work up his nerve just to talk to her. Even then, she almost had to ask *him* if they could go out and do something together.

Their courtship was slow and steady, pretty nontraditional in this fast-paced culture. We admired Brian because of his commitment to our daughter and because of his personal purity and honesty.

Eventually the day arrived when Amy told us, "Brian is going to ask me to marry him—I just know he is!" Yet literally months went by and he didn't ask. Still, Amy knew the question was coming. "He's going to ask you guys for permission to marry me," she told us. But he didn't. Finally we started saying things like, "Brian, is there *anything else* we need to talk about?" He knew what we were trying to pull out of him, but he just wasn't ready to say those words. These days he'll admit he was scared to death of me (I have no idea why). I guess that's the normal way of things. I remember being mighty nervous around Nancy's dad all the time; and now here he was, driving the van on my cross-country adventure. It works out in the end.

Getting Our "Kicks" on . . .

Everyone in the desert needs one thing: water. By the time we had biked eighty-eight miles, we really needed some. The first place we stopped was run by a family who spoke almost no English. We couldn't communicate what we wanted and left as parched as when we'd arrived. In Pear Blossom we found a little cafe and success. The friendly folks there gave us water and our first directions from "locals," and we discovered that one of the principles we'd learned about was absolutely true: When it comes to giving directions and estimating mileage, locals tend to think in terms of cars, not bikes.

One very large man suggested that we take another route because Highway 138 was so busy. "Is it any longer?" I asked. The man pondered the question and replied, "Well, I think it's about the same." Pause. "I don't know."

Of course, another mile on a bike is something to avoid. In Acton we had asked our waitress how far it was to the next town, and she replied in terms familiar to most of us: "It's about an hour." That is, an hour *by car*. What we really wanted to know was how many miles was it to the next town. Distance in miles is vitally important when you're traveling from city to city on a bike, especially with the wind in your face.

We had battled just such a wind most of the day, but when we turned onto Highway 18 into Victorville, we expected some relief. The wind should finally be at our backs. We pushed hard for that moment, eagerly anticipating it. Yet when the moment arrived, we discovered road crews had begun resurfacing the pavement. All the old blacktop had been ripped up and repaving had not yet begun. We ended up riding two and half miles on a road that couldn't get much rougher. We went from wind in our faces to washboard road. Of course, a little thing like that didn't stop the cars from flying along at breakneck speed. Airborne pebbles hit Brian several times. (A few bees and even a tumbleweed had attacked him earlier in the day; he must have some kind of scent that I lack. Praise the Lord.)

With thirty-three miles to go before we reached Barstow, Brian and I turned on to Historic Route 66 just out of Victorville. Once known as "The Main Street of America," old Route 66 began at the corner of Jackson Boulevard and Michigan Avenue in Chicago and wound 2,400 miles across America through eight states and three time zones to Santa Monica, California. It was America's first continuously paved link between Los Angeles and Chicago and the shortest all-weather route between those two cities.

From 1926 to 1984, U.S. Route 66 was one of America's primary east-west arteries, linking hundreds of cities and towns. The highway got a tremendous boost from President Franklin D. Roosevelt's New Deal. Due in large part to the Civilian Conservation Corps (CCC) and Works Project Administration (WPA), Route 66 was finally "continuously paved" by 1938. At the height of its popularity just after World War II, millions of Americans followed Route 66 to new lives in the West. But the war signaled the beginning of the end for the highway. Before the war, when Dwight D. Eisenhower was a young captain, he found his command bogged down in spring mud near Ft. Riley, Kansas, while on a coast-to-coast maneuver. He never forgot it. Years later, after General Eisenhower returned from Germany, he noted the strategic value of Hitler's autobahn: "During World War II, I saw the superlative system of German national highways crossing that country and offering the possibility, often lacking in the United States, to drive with speed and safety at the same time."[1] At his urging, the Federal Highway Act of 1956 underwrote the cost of constructing a national interstate system. And by October 1984 the final section of the original Route 66 was replaced by Interstate 40 at Williams, Arizona.

My personal memories of Route 66 date back forty-five years to when my family traveled from California to Virginia for summer vacations. One day in Needles, on the California-Arizona border, the daytime temperature rose to more than a hundred degrees and it didn't cool down below ninety at night. We'd stay in six and eight dollar motels with no air conditioning or water cooler and endure a miserable sleep.

Much of the present old Route 66 evokes little of the nostalgia suggested by books and songs. Instead, decay and ruin extend their destructive tentacles everywhere. Outside of Oro Grande, dilapidated little shanties made of wood or stucco or stone stand as mute sentinels and reminders of better days. Wind blows through paneless windows, flapping tattered drapes. Old cars rust in the open. Scores of abandoned buildings and gas stations in various stages of disintegration fall back into the earth.

In the midst of the crumbling buildings and faded signs as the hot air blew against my face seemingly propelled by the bellows of Hell, I realized that "Jesus Christ is the same yesterday and today and forever" (Heb. 13:8). While everything we build eventually collapses into disrepair and ruin, "I the LORD do not change" (Mal. 3:6). While celebrated manmade works return to dust, "the word of our God stands forever" (Isa. 40:8). And although our most cherished accomplishments wrinkle and fade and pass away, "the man who does the will of God lives forever" (1 John 2:17).

Comforting thoughts as we pulled into a warm Barstow at 7:00 P.M., our second day of riding at last complete. We had biked our first century, 108 miles, much of it against twenty-five mile-per-hour winds that dropped us down to a pedaling speed of nine miles per hour. At times like that it's easy to give in to the temptation to give up, to quit. When I began training for this trip, there was a time that I'd be climbing a steep hill and I would get tired and say, "I need to stop. I just can't go on." And I'd quit. That is, until I had a crucial conversation with Tom Ritchey.

I was telling him about my progress and said, "The biggest barrier, the biggest hurdle that I feel I have and have always had is my stamina."

"It's all in your mind, Mike," he explained. "Your body is sending you some physical messages that your mind blows out of proportion. So you stop. If you will just push through those first times when your body starts to say, 'I'm breathing so hard I can't keep going,' then you will send a little message to your brain that you *can* keep going. Then your brain will play a game back with your body and say, 'The next time you try to send that message, are you sure?' You'll have this ping-pong thing going until finally you'll either have gone farther than you thought you could go and you will stop once more, or you won't stop—and you'll never stop again. Once you push through it, you will have not only climbed that hurdle, you will have knocked it down. And you won't have to go over it again."

Tom was absolutely right. Not once on the entire ride across the country did Brian or I stop out of sheer fatigue. I learned that I needed to push through tough times, to refuse to give in to my body simply because it was tired. You know, sometimes all we need is just one solitary voice saying, "Yes, you can. Yes, you can." We all need somebody to encourage us in that way. That's what Tom did for me.

Entering the Desert

May 12 looked to be one of the toughest rides of our trip. We needed to bike forty miles into Ludlow, then get as close to Needles as possible, another ninety-five miles away. All of that would take us through the heart of the Mojave Desert.

When you hear the word "desert," what comes to mind? Most folks probably imagine a barren wasteland, impossibly hot, covered in sand and rocks and inhospitable to nearly all forms of life.

But that's not the Mojave!

Sure, it's hot; the temperature averaged above 110 degrees in our trek across it. And yes there is sand and much rocky terrain. But lifeless? Hardly.

The most ubiquitous resident of the Mojave, a settler that almost defines its boundaries, is the Joshua tree. The Joshua tree is one of about thirty species of yuccas, all native to North America. And it's *strange*. Lieutenant John C. Fremont crossed the Mojave with Kit Carson in 1844 and wrote in his diary about Joshua trees, "their stiff and ungraceful form makes them to the traveler the most repulsive tree in the vegetable kingdom."[2] Even accomplished and noteworthy botanists call the Joshua tree "weird-looking." Susan D. McKelvey, author of *Yuccas of the Southwestern United States,* called the Joshua tree "a curious looking plant, suggesting in its oldest forms especially, another age; one would not be surprised to see a huge prehistoric monster standing by and feeding upon the fruit on its upper branches."[3]

From a distance the gnarled and twisted plant appears to be coated with furry armor. It grows from fifteen to forty feet high and produces whitish flowers in the spring that feel rubbery and smell vaguely like mushrooms.

While the Joshua tree may be the Mojave's most peculiar resident, it's far from the only one. Plants such as the Parry saltbush, Panamint parsley, and Telescope Peak buckwheat are found only in the Mojave, and only in its driest pockets. The Mojave also harbors various species of cactus, including the Bigelow cholla, also called the teddybear or jumping cholla. It grows to twelve feet in height and has a thick main trunk with large "chains" of spiny arms clustering on the branches. The plant's dead buds are said to "jump" when they pop off the plant, making them one of the desert's most dangerous organisms. "One doesn't mess with these chollas," one author wrote. "They get their moniker as jumpers because of their propensity for breaking off, when touched, at a joint in the 'chain.' The joint is then attached, by means of formidable spines, to any luckless critter that brushes against it, be he man or beast. Once imbedded, a cholla spine is difficult to remove. But this is all quite in keeping with the tenacity of desert life—success in the desert is measured in adaptation and resourcefulness, and this is just the cholla's way of propagating itself."[4]

On our trek through the desert we also saw several lizards and many ants, flies, and flying insects. Various creatures skittered across the road and as I looked out on this hot, blazing desert, I thought, *There's a whole world of life out there in what appears to be an uninhabitable desert. Plants live there, animals live there; who knows what else exists among the rocks and holes of the Mojave?*

Then I thought of the neighborhoods and communities in which we all live. When I was growing up, we knew all of our neighbors. We'd often get together with them and considered them close friends. That's no longer true for most of us. We're a transient people and we don't stay too long in any one place. Our lives have become more hectic, moving in a bewildering number of directions. We're involved in this and busy with that and we don't even meet our neighbors, let alone know them.

Just like the Mojave, there are whole worlds all around us about which we know next to nothing. People are hurt, they're getting divorced, their children are in trouble. We see emergency vehicles scream through the neighborhood and we may ask a question or two, but no more. We just don't get to know the folks around us.

In my own neighborhood we did have a man across the street who was the neighborhood gadfly. I think every neighborhood ought to have one. He pulled everyone together; he was the drawstring for the street. He would put together barbecues during the summer and potluck dinners during the winter and invite everyone in the neighborhood over to eat. If someone was moving, he'd organize a goodbye party. He's no longer there, and he's missed. I know how important it is to create such neighborhood activities, but I have not been good at it.

Part of the problem may be that those of us who count ourselves Christians oftentimes gravitate toward fellow Christians and exclude those who aren't. I know of one man who was asked to consider putting together a Christmas party for residents of his neighborhood. "But—but they're not Christians!" he objected.

"I know; that's the point," explained a friend.

The party never happened. We tend to stick close to those who are like us rather than reaching out to those whose lifestyles and beliefs differ from our own.

But what wonders would we discover if we broadened our horizons and made an effort to get to know our neighbors? How would our own narrow lives be enriched by showing a genuine interest in the foreign worlds of those who live right next door to us? The Mojave taught me that those worlds are worth observing, appreciating, and even exploring. And the only thing that keeps me from doing so is an errant belief that they're all lifeless deserts.

They're not. And I've got some work to do.

Lost and Found

A few miles outside of Daggett, our van lost contact with us. According to Ted and Steve, one moment we were riding on the highway, and the next moment we had disappeared. Gone. Dematerialized. And not for a few moments, but for a couple of hours. By 11:00 A.M., they still could find no sign of Brian and me and were beginning to get worried. They began to scour the countryside for us, first driving a few miles up the highway, then doubling back to make sure they hadn't missed us. After a few of these search missions without spotting us, they visited a rest stop to check the facilities. No sign of us. They pulled off the road to check a likely spot. Nothing. They climbed a hill to scan the area from a better viewpoint. Still nothing. Most disturbing of all, the cellular phone remained silent. No calls from us, and they couldn't raise us.

My father-in-law Ted was especially concerned. He didn't want to even think about the worst, but he knew it was a possibility. They were about to call the state police when the van phone rang. It was Donna Lewis, my capable assistant at Focus on the Family.

"Steve?" she said. "This is Donna. Mike called me and wanted me to tell you that he and Brian are in Ludlow at a cafe there. They're having lunch."

They immediately drove to Ludlow, relieved to see us, but pretty eager for our explanation. After all, we had caused them a couple of frantic hours. Our explanation was quite simple, actually. When people talk about old Route 66, they ought to emphasize the *old*. I don't know when the section out of Barstow was last paved, but some of its grooves and potholes went so deep I think I could see the asphalt my family rode on back in the 1950s. It still was down there somewhere, and my bike tire was touching it. Before we hit these rough stretches of road we were averaging sixteen to eighteen miles per hour with a nice breeze at our backs, but the wretched road forced us to drop down to six or seven miles per hour—and *still* we felt as if we were being pounded to death.

We finally decided that the bikes were getting beaten up, so we cut over to Interstate 40, where we made excellent time. We zipped through one construction area where the workers seemed friendly enough, so we kept going. Unfortunately I had left my cellular phone in the van when we left that morning and had no way to communicate with our "partners."

Big mistake. I violated a concept that had been drilled into me during my years with Focus on the Family: accountability. Don't be a lone wolf. Keep everything out in the open. One of the primary reasons Dr. Dobson's ministry has survived rocket-like growth is its strong system of accountability throughout management. Checks and balances are everywhere, and each person has the right to question whether an issue has been handled properly.

On this day I also violated a key part of our on-the-road accountability system, namely to keep one another apprised of our whereabouts. Seeing the concern on Ted's face that day in the Ludlow Cafe hammered the lesson home like a firm scolding!

This is Home

Ludlow was established in the late 1800s as a water stop for the railroad. There's not much there anymore; these days it's pretty much a water stop for bikers. Still, it was a nicer little town than I had expected. The people there enjoy life in a small desert community off the beaten path. They obviously take pride in what they do.

"Why in the world would someone choose to live out in a place like this?" I asked our waitress, a middle-aged woman.

"Hey, this is home," she replied. "I like it out here." This was a refrain we heard often across America. Home is important to people. A sense of place. Belonging. People need to feel that connection with the land, whether it's a tiny town in the middle of the desert or a neighborhood in the shadows of skyscrapers.

While we waited for our lunch to be served, another patron noticed our biking garb and approached our table.

"Are you guys bicyclists?" he asked.

"Why, yes we are," I replied.

"Your clothes look like it," he said. "Are they comfortable?"

"They're made especially for biking," I responded. "I don't think I'd like to wear the spandex shorts to a business meeting."

After a few more questions he paused, looked us over once more, and said, "You *are* who I thought you were, then. You're Mike Trout from *Focus on the Family*, aren't you?"

Our new friend, Frank Andrews, had heard about our trip on a radio station in San Diego and just wanted to say hello. That's right—San Diego. So what was he doing out in Ludlow?

"I'm taking my mother to Joplin, Missouri, so she can see her youngest granddaughter graduate from high school," he explained.

I was impressed. "That kind of thing just doesn't happen too much anymore these days," I told him. We hear so much about older Americans being ignored or even mistreated by their adult children, making Frank's pilgrimage refreshing indeed.

All too soon, Brian and I had to bid our new friends goodbye and head back out on the asphalt ribbon stretching across the Mojave. We settled into a pace that seemed comfortable enough, but sooner than we expected I was beginning to tire. The unrelenting sun was baking the life out of me, and I knew I wouldn't be able to go much farther without taking a break. But since we had to cover a lot of miles, we pressed on. Stamina. Willpower. Mind over matter. Prayer. We reached deep for every resource we could muster, but by 3:00 P.M. I was out of gas. I cleared some space in the back of the van, laid down, closed my eyes, and just sort of moaned. I was concerned about the sun and possible heat prostration; I know how it sneaks up on you. And while I had been drinking a lot of water, still the sun can heat your body to dangerous levels. I didn't feel especially bad, just tired. I thought fifteen minutes of rest should do the trick.

But it was not to be. After only five minutes, the phone rang. Have you seen that cellular phone commercial where the boss calls back to his partying employees at the office? Well, that's sort of how I felt when I heard Dr. Dobson's voice on the other end. He wanted to do our first on-the-road interview, but he caught me flat on my back. I took the call, but our connection left a lot to be desired:

Interview One

Dobson: We have just placed a call to Mike and I believe he's on the line. Mike, where in the world are you?

Trout: This won't mean anything to you, but I'm about twenty miles east of Ludlow, California, on my way to Needles across the Mojave Desert—it was 109 degrees last we checked.

Dobson: So you're talking to us on a little hand-held phone in the middle of the desert.

Trout: I am right next to Interstate 40, the trucks and the cars are flyin' by, and it's hotter than a pistol out here.

Dobson: Well, your voice sounds very much like Edward R. Murrow in 1942, telling us about the Battle of Britain.

Trout: I feel like I'm on the moon, reporting back from some lunar surface somewhere.

Dobson: Do I understand that you've been lying flat on your back with your legs in the air, complaining about cramps?

Trout: No, I haven't, but it's been a tiring day. We did 108 miles yesterday and stayed in Barstow, California, and we're going to try and make it to Needles, which is about 140 miles. I'm not sure we'll make it. But we *had* just taken a break when you called, so your timing is perfect.

Dobson: Do you have wind in your face?

Trout: We've had the wind at our back most of the day today and we've been able to average about fifteen to eighteen miles an hour. However, it's just turned and it's in our face now. We've been climbing a hill for almost twenty miles and it looks like we may be close to the top, so that will be the best news we've had.

Dobson: A twenty-mile hill! Would you tell our listeners one more time why you're doing this?

Trout: I think mainly for the adventure, and so far I've had a lot of it. I met our first *Focus* listener today in the Ludlow Cafe. There's only a Chevron station, a motel, and a cafe in Ludlow. A gentleman was paying his bill and he looked over at the table at us sitting there having lunch, and he walked over and introduced himself and said, "I *thought* you were Mike Trout! I heard the conversation with you and Dr. Dobson about this trip on the air. I live in San Diego and I'm taking my mother to Joplin, Missouri, to see her oldest granddaughter graduate from high school. And here we are, and how nice to talk to you."

Dobson: You welcome people to say hello to you along the way, don't you?

Trout: Oh, absolutely! I really want to talk to people. We saw a man walking along the side of the road as we left Barstow and asked him where he was going. He said he was walking home. "Boy, it's awfully hot to be out walking," we replied, and he said, "But it beats the air in Los Angeles. It's nicer out here than it is in L.A."

Dobson: Tell us real quickly, Mike, where you will be along the way on Tuesday.

Trout: As I said, we hope to make it as far as Needles, California, today. That's right on the Colorado River. I doubt if we'll do that; we'll probably get almost there and ride in the van the rest of the way and then come back and ride in on the next day. But we'll go through Needles and on over to Williams, Arizona, and maybe just a little north of there as we head up toward Colorado.

Dobson:	Are you having a good time, Mike?
Trout:	You know, we *have* had a good time. The weather, as I said, is very hot today, but it was pleasant yesterday. We had some strong wind in our faces and that made it miserable for a while, but cloud cover helped and we really have done pretty well. As the wind turns around and gets to your back, it makes the ride very, very comfortable. So we've had a good time so far.
Dobson:	Well, we'll try to keep up with you, Mike, and we'll give you a call every day or two and let our listeners know where you are.
Trout:	Great! And I look forward to seeing a lot of them along the way.

It wasn't surprising, I suppose. We were dead center in the middle of the Mojave Desert with civilization nowhere in sight. I was amazed we got any kind of signal at all. Still, Dr. Dobson was right about the poor quality of the sound. That's why I signed off by saying, "This is Mike Trout reporting from the Mojave Desert," as if I were a war correspondent from fifty years ago.

My only real war, however, was the battle to get as close to Needles as we could manage by the end of the day. At 3:30 P.M., that fight heated up again.

The next few hours were pretty uneventful. About the only sign of civilization I saw was some graffiti on a bridge that read, "Dave loves Lydia." It looked as if it had been there for a couple of years, and I wondered if Dave *still* loves Lydia. The miles crept by, taking us farther and farther into the desert, which seemed to change hues almost by the minute.

At 6:00 P.M. we waved the white flag of surrender. We were about forty-five miles outside of Needles, our anticipated destination. But we had ridden 102 miles in the most intense heat we'd face on the entire trip, and we didn't melt. The day was everything I had anticipated it would be and a little more. It was an encouraging day. We did it! We made it! And we were still able to walk.

I had at least one major concern when I started out on this trip. Would I be able to finish? Could I make it all the way? I recalled vividly one afternoon several weeks earlier when Marlen Wells had come down to ride with me for several hours. We climbed some pretty steep inclines and when we returned home, Marlen said, "You're ready." Marlen is a wonderful encourager and will occasionally say things that lean more toward optimism than truth. However, that day he spoke with such firm conviction that I accepted his evaluation. He'll never know the strength and confidence I drew from those few words—and how many times along our trip I replayed them in my mind.

If you want to exercise a healthy influence over someone, shower them with positive and encouraging words! I appreciated Brian's company for the same reason, because he's an encourager, too. His neck hurt when my neck hurt and his back ached when my back ached, but sometimes one of us felt good when the other didn't—and so we supported each other. He told me to drink water, and I told him to slow down.

Free Ice Cream!

The late, legendary coach of the Green Bay Packers, Vince Lombardi, once said, "Fatigue makes cowards of us all." The next morning we felt more tired than we had thus far on the trip. Fatigue was rearing its ugly head. This was the first morning in which both Brian and I said, "You know what? I could go back to bed right now."

Eventually we got on the road. Moments later we suffered our third flat tire in four days. Another flat followed about an hour later. We made it to the top of a big hill made lovely by a yellow sign bearing delectable news: "Down grade. Watch for slow vehicles." But we also encountered a frustrating headwind. Unfair!

By midafternoon we pulled into a Texaco station blaring the news, "FREE ICE CREAM CONE with 8 gallon fillup." Yes, Virginia, we are in the Mojave. We know it not only by the station's ice cream enticements but also by the flat tires that multiply in this unbearable heat. Just two miles outside of Needles, Brian got another one. If you're keeping score, that's three for the day.

Yet not all our unscheduled stops were unpleasant. At an underpass on Interstate 40, we met Cyle G. Davis. Cyle was resting inside his car with the windows rolled down.

"Are you OK?" I asked.

"Yes," he said, "I'm just tired and was afraid I was going to fall asleep at the wheel. I thought I'd better stop."

Cyle looks to be in his seventies and, judging by his rugged hands, he's done some good, hard labor in his life. His well-worn clothes speak the same message.

"Where'd you come from?" I asked.

"I flew into Los Angeles from Santiago, Chile," he replied.

"Really? Why were you there?"

Now I don't want to make too much of this, but what are the odds of stumbling upon a ministry under an overpass in the Mojave Desert?

"Well, for forty years I served as a missionary with the Assemblies of God. By Chilean law the schools must teach religion, so these days I build schools. Then missionaries come to teach the students about Christianity. Whoever builds the school controls what religion is taught, and I think it's a pretty effective ministry. I just finished one school that's as large as a square city block. It has about 2,000 students."

Cyle was headed back to Springfield, Missouri, to visit his family, and the differences between the nation he had just left and ours startled him. He shook his head and wondered out loud where we were going as a country.

"Kids today in the U.S. can't even say the word 'Jesus Christ' with respect," he said. "It's nothing more to them than a swear word. Yet in Chile they mandate by law that you teach religion on the school campus."

Cyle and I had a great but brief time of Christian fellowship under that bridge, but all too soon it was time to climb back on the bike. As I left the shady sanctuary, Cyle hollered out to us, "Thanks. You've helped me clear my head. I feel wide awake now."

Ten seconds later he passed Brian and me and honked his horn, continuing his long drive home in his vintage '80s Buick.

Poetic Evangelism

You meet the neatest people when you walk into a small town restaurant in biker shorts. Automatic conversation starters, these outfits of ours. At the California Pantry in Needles, we met

Richard Drake, a local Sunday school director who makes his living as a night waterman for a nearby golf course. Richard has four daughters and told us he has "been back with the Lord for two years." When he found out what we were doing and that I worked with *Focus on the Family,* he shook my hand vigorously and said, "I just want to let you know that there are Christians out here and we want to encourage you."

After wishing us well he excused himself, only to reappear a few minutes later. This time he was carrying gifts for everyone in our group: beautifully framed poetry he had written himself. Richard has composed more than two hundred poems and is trying to get them published. The following piece he calls "The Great I Am."

> *Let the Spirit guide us*
> *Let the Spirit show*
> *Let the Spirit teach us*
> *All we need to know.*
> *What we need is Jesus*
> *What we need is love*
> *What we need is only found*
> *In our God above.*
> *Pray the Lord for patience*
> *Pray the Lord for peace*
> *Pray the Lord to show us how*
> *To make selfish desires cease.*
> *Worthy is our Savior*
> *Worthy is the Lamb*
> *Worthy is the Son of Man*
> *He is the Great I Am!*

After reciting from memory one of his poems that he said was "especially in his heart" and peppering his conversation with the phrase "Praise God," Richard once more shook our hands and said good-bye. "It's a blessing to meet with you," he said as he left for the final time.

Watching the door close, I thought Richard was sent to us for encouragement. Here we were in a small town in the desert and I "happen" to run into a guy who expresses his faith by writing poetry. My hunch is that Richard probably does not have a degree in literature, and he probably hasn't attended many poetry-writing workshops. But he loves the Lord and can't contain the stirring in his soul, so out comes his praise and adoration in poetry.

I'm reminded of an old story about the evangelist D. L. Moody. Someone confronted him one day on the street about his evangelism methods. "You don't like the way I do evangelism?" Moody asked. "To be honest, neither do I. But I like my way of doing evangelism better than your way of not doing it." Richard does evangelism in the way God has equipped him, and I'm grateful for it.

That night we stayed in Needles at a Super 8 motel owned by Ed and Linda Davenport, a couple who also pastor Southwest Christian Center, a church in Lake Havasu City, Arizona. The Davenports have owned the motel off and on since the late 1970s and make outstanding hosts. They donated our night's lodging and gave us a great place to rest. Ed has a sort of an ex-Marine appearance—short haircut and a stocky, powerful build. He looks as if he ought to be yelling out orders to new recruits at boot camp rather than sharing the gospel with a quivering voice. In my mind, his physical appearance didn't match what he truly is—and that's a testimony to what Christ can do with any of us.

It was wonderful to stay with a generous Christian couple dedicated to serving God wherever he calls them. Throughout our trip we were indebted to the gracious hospitality of men and women to whom we had no connection other than our mutual commitment to Jesus Christ. But what a connection! Even in the midst of the Mojave Desert, under blazing skies and baking temperatures, choice servants of the living God do what they can to assist his struggling children and thereby glorify him. Although I hadn't covered that much territory, the heart of America was looking a lot different from what I saw on television and in the newspapers.

CHAPTER 3

Nothing Much
But Staggering Beauty

By crossing the Colorado River outside of Needles, California, and thereby entering Arizona on the morning of May 14, we could officially claim that our trip had become an interstate affair. Since we knew it was going to be another blazing day—the expected high was again 110 degrees—we got on the road by 7:45 A.M. to get moving toward Truxton, Arizona.

Our four days in Arizona would present us with some of the most spectacular scenery of our adventure. Gaping canyons, towering buttes, soaring mesas, rugged volcanic peaks, breathtaking limestone cliffs and sheer walls of red rock would provide a stunning backdrop for the saguaro cacti and delicate wildflowers that bloomed with vibrant color along the highway.

We rode old Route 66 most of the day and, once again, rolling along on this portion of old highway brought back some wonderful memories. No doubt we had cruised this very pavement in the '50s on our family vacations. Perry Como probably crooned on the AM radio and my two sisters and I were surely already asking if we were "there" yet. Mom never learned to drive, so Dad stood watch behind the wheel, mile after mile. At the end of a fourteen-hour day, he would peel his fingers off that old plastic steering wheel, stretch the cramps out of his legs and back, and proclaim that his eyes felt as if they'd been worked over with sandpaper. I can't imagine the fatigue he must have felt.

Our vacations lasted only two weeks, and more than half of that time was spent getting there or coming home! But at least the journey could be made inexpensively. Gas cost less than twenty-five cents a gallon back then, acceptable overnight lodging could be found for under ten dollars, and meals were prepared in advance and eaten in the car or in a park. If we stopped at a restaurant, the bill seldom came to more than six or seven bucks. Round trip, we probably spent less than two hundred dollars!

Still, that was a lot of money to my parents. It was a real sacrifice for them to give us a few rushed days with relatives and friends. But oh, the memories I have of warm Virginia summer nights, screened porches, and lightning bugs! They were worth every scorching mile of the ride! Younger parents have told me that it's hard to get away for family vacations, but I strongly urge you to do it. Your kids might initially whine about having to ride long distances in the car and be away from their friends, but just you wait: once they leave the nest they'll thank you for those times together.

Flat Tires and Hungry Burros

The longest uninterrupted remaining stretch of old Route 66 lies in Arizona, stretching from Topoc, just south of Needles, to Seligman, a distance of some 160 miles. Travelers to this remote area are not only invited to drink in its stark beauty but also are warned about some of its dangers. One sign advised us that "in mountain driving, always expect a vehicle around the next bend, and yield the right of way to uphill traffic. Be on the lookout for wild burros and bighorn sheep in the road. Caution when exploring by foot. This section of Historic Route 66 is riddled with open mineshafts which can be deep and dangerous."

We never left the road, but even we could see the wisdom of such advice. "White Chief Mine—Keep Out!" shouted one quickly scrawled poster jammed between a crevice in the rocks. Yet mines aren't the only dangers in the area. For bicyclists, far more troublesome are the sharp wires left behind on the road from shredded, steel-belted tires. One of these wires punctured Brian's back tire. Repairs took nearly half an hour because we accidentally punctured the new tube while inserting it and had to redo the whole thing. All three of our flats the day before and this one were caused by the carcasses of steel-belted tires.

An hour before high noon we arrived in Oatman, Arizona, a tourist's version of an Old West ghost town. A sign outside of town encourages visitors to step back in time, feed the wild burros, and patronize the local shops. And wild burros really do run free through the streets. Long ago their ancestors were domesticated, but these animals belong to no one but themselves and they wander through town, looking for handouts. We fed one old boy a Peak Bar and snapped a picture we might later sell to the manufacturer for promotional purposes. He appeared to like it (although he seemed no more energetic after eating it than he did before—a fact we won't share with Real Good Food, the bars' maker).

We were surprised at the number of foreign tourists in little, out-of-the-way Oatman—scads of visitors from France, Germany, Italy, and the Pacific Rim. This area, especially the Grand Canyon, is heavily promoted in Europe and Asia. We spoke briefly to a Frenchman who lives just outside of Paris.

"What sort of gearing have you on the bike?" he asked.

"I haven't been asked that before—were you ever in the Tour de France?" I replied.

With a laugh in his voice he said, "I wasn't in the Tour de France, but I'm very familiar with bike riding. I live in hilly country—so I am surprised you don't have different gearing for these mountains."

Our bikes were geared for general conditions and not specifically for climbing mountains, and our French friend could hardly believe it. But that wasn't the only thing he had a hard time believing. He was also amazed that we would tackle a trip like ours in such weather.

"One hundred miles in this sun? Crazy! I wish you luck."

Just outside Oatman we ascended nearly two thousand feet in just three miles. Without question it was our toughest climb to date. A number of times the incline to Sitgreaves Pass was so steep we could barely stand up on our bikes and use all our weight to force the pedals into giving us just one more revolution. Normally we planned our route so that we paralleled a railroad grade, whose pitches seldom exceed four or five percent. The road to Sitgreaves, however, approached twelve percent in several places (and felt straight up).

The most difficult "official" climb in American bicycle racing is up Mount Mitchell in North Carolina. The grueling push to the 6,684 foot summit (the highest point east of the Rockies) takes riders through the center of the Blue Ridge Mountains and features some "heart thumping" sections with punishing twenty percent grades in the last few miles. It takes a seasoned athlete who has trained long hours on steep terrain to enjoy these classic climbs. I was still working on the seasoning!

How wonderful it felt finally to pause by the sign that confirmed we had reached the 3,550-foot summit of Sitgreaves Pass! My sense of accomplishment could not be doused even by the perspiration drenching my body. Another milestone had been passed! If you're a "to-do list" person, you understand the high one gets as each item gets checked off.

On our way to Kingman we came upon hundreds of saguaro cacti raising their spiny arms to the sky, proclaiming their mastery of the desert and, perhaps, petitioning for a little moisture. The saguaro can grow to sixty feet in height, has up to five or six branches, and produces white, night-blooming flowers when the plant reaches fifty to seventy-five years of age—blooms that are the state flower of Arizona.

The saguaro is a protected plant species, but that doesn't stop some miscreants from removing them from their natural desert habitat or otherwise harming them. Legal penalties are stiff for damaging a wild saguaro, but none is so severe as the one I heard about recently on one of those "news of the unusual" features. It seems a young man decided to flout the law by taking his rifle out to the desert for some target practice. After firing several shots at a huge old saguaro, he approached the cactus to inspect his marksmanship—whereupon the weakened giant toppled over on the doomed lawbreaker, killing him instantly. The story came out when the young man's desiccated body was discovered a few days after the accident. Moral of the tale: If you crave a little target practice, hunt up some old pop cans. But stay away from the saguaros! Those wily cacti will get you if the law doesn't.

Road Warrior

We saw him from far away, his knees pumping slowly and methodically, his creaking bicycle loaded down as if it were a mechanical pack mule. At first we thought we were seeing an elderly man—from a distance his mostly gray hair and wild, unruly beard appeared to belong to a man in his seventies. But Rodney Jones is not in his seventies; if he's yet reached his fortieth birthday, I'd be surprised. It's just that the few years he's collected have been pretty hard on him.

We met Rodney a few miles outside of Kingman. He was dressed in long, dark pants and a heavy shirt and spoke carefully and economically, like a man who has spent much of his time alone. In Rodney's case, appearances are not at all deceiving.

"I've been biking for fifteen months," Rodney told us. "I started out in Missouri and have been to about fifteen states so far."

Rodney collects cans in each new city he visits, turns them in for scrap money, and then moves on.

"I don't like this bike here," he said, pointing a bony finger to his creaking conveyance, his third. "It don't carry weight well. I lost my last one in San Jose" (he didn't explain what he meant by "lost"). We offered Rodney some water and other liquids, which he greedily and thankfully accepted. Then we asked how he came to be in the searing Arizona sun on his way to nowhere in particular.

"I was married," he began, "but things just didn't work out. Me and the wife decided to move to another state to see if things would get better, but they didn't. So we moved to Missouri. But that didn't work out either."

He paused briefly, then said in a slow, measured voice, "Finally the old lady stopped cleaning the house, welfare took the kids, and I figured it was time to get out of there." And that's when he hopped on a bike. He's been pedaling across the country ever since.

I was stunned. "Well, how long do you think you'll keep this up?" I asked.

"I figure I'll stop when I die," Rodney answered without hesitation.

What a devastatingly sad comment! My conversation with Rodney revealed him to be an "ordinary" enough fellow, not wildly unstable or psychotic or mentally challenged. And that bothered me even more. *Rodney is not too different from me,* I thought, *and yet we meet in the middle of the Arizona desert, our life perspectives whole worlds—no, galaxies; no, universes—apart. What accounts for that difference?*

I believe it was writer Norman Cousins who said something like, "A man can live ten minutes without air, two days without water, and forty days without food—but not a single second without hope." No wonder God calls hope the "anchor for the soul" (see Heb. 6:19). Lose that anchor and the ship of your life will drift aimlessly out into a vast, brutal, unending sea.

Hope has unquenchable power, and I pray that someday Rodney will discover its warm embrace. If you see him along the road, offer him a cup of cold water in the name of Christ, will you?

Heard Any Good Jokes?

In Kingman we asked a local bike shop owner where we could get a good, late lunch, and he recommended the Mexican restaurant next door, El Palacio. In addition to seeking fine food, Brian also sought a good joke. Every morning on the radio he was supposed to be ready with a backslapper to tickle the funny bone of the station's audience, and he searched for them wherever we went.

Most of them were real groaners. Such as:

Q: What do you call a beetle on a motorcycle?

A: Evil boll weevil.

And ...

A blind man walks into a department store and starts swinging his seeing-eye dog around. The clerk says, "Hey, buddy, what are you doing? Can I help you?" The blind man says, "No, thanks. I'm just taking a look around."

Try as we might, we couldn't coax a joke out of our waitress, which was too bad because *anything* would have been better than the ones Brian was coming up with! We finished our meal—so far, the best one of the trip—and headed out the door and onto our bikes. The next several miles passed uneventfully, and before we knew it we were riding in the coolness of a beautiful late afternoon that was quickly turning into early evening. For forty miles or so we cruised over smooth roads and enjoyed a marvelous time. Those moments had a surreal feel to them. Very few cars lumbered past and at times it felt as though we were the only two people on the earth. As the sun sank behind us, the desert colors leaped to vivid life and the outline of the distant horizon appeared freshly painted. This was a peaceful and refreshing time, the kind of afternoon I envisioned as I planned the trip. We passed an old gas station, long since abandoned. It demanded a Kodak moment, so we took turns snapping pictures. We also used this quiet break to have our first thoughtful conversation, this middle-aged guy and his son-in-law.

When Brian entered our lives, I didn't think so much about releasing a daughter as I thought about gaining a son, a son I'd never had. I thought about the things that we would do together as father-in-law and son. And now one of those moments was happening.

The thing I most like about Brian is his respect, for which his parents can be praised. He responds to me just as a good son ought to respond to a father-in-law. He asks a lot of questions. He's all ears; he loves to listen. And he loves to discuss anything and everything, from bicycle maintenance to desert flora to the best car to purchase. For a long time that evening we enjoyed good conversation. The trains ran by us so we talked about the influence of railroads as they surged across the country. We talked about desert weather. We dreamed about where we'd like to live if we could live anywhere we pleased. We discussed road conditions and weather patterns and sports. And we talked a lot about life plans.

Once Brian committed his life to Christ, he began to take a completely fresh look at his future. He had always planned on being a physical therapist and therefore became a biology major. But after his conversion he realized he would rather work in some form of ministry with young kids. "What is it like to be a part of a ministry?" he asked. "What does it feel like?" "What is it like working for a nonprofit organization?" "What do you think about my strengths?" "What kind of future is there in ministry as a career?" Whoa! Slow down. But actually, his questions gave me a great opportunity to share how God not only gave me a gift and a love for radio but helped me see how I could use it to serve him. We sometimes think that in order to serve God we need to go off on some heroic mission, but I believe God has a plan for us that is linked very closely to our special abilities and interests. Of course, we need to be open to *anything* God asks of us, but in his great wisdom he always calls us to do the very things that he has equipped us to do. In other words, he doesn't ask someone who can't carry a tune in a bushel basket to sing in the church choir. (Some choir members should reread these last two sentences.)

We also talked theology. That morning as we were retrieving the bikes from the van, two men got out of a car and walked toward us, their hands stuffed with literature. Prior to approaching us they had gone truck to truck at a nearby truckstop-restaurant, witnessing to anyone who would listen (few did). Now they were going to witness to the bikers. Immediately we identified them as members of Jehovah's Witnesses. They offered the usual small talk and then wanted to show us their magazine *The Watchtower*. We thanked them for their interest and told them we were with Focus on the Family; they didn't know what that was, but as soon as they heard it was a Christian ministry, they turned, wished us well, and that was the end of that.

The brief encounter did, however, provide a springboard for discussion between Brian and me about theology and cults and the difference between various denominations. What makes a group like the Jehovah's Witnesses a cult? Why do so many cults deny the Trinity? Practically all groups claim the Bible is their guide in spiritual matters, so why is there so much disagreement over what it says? How does an average person know what the Scriptures really teach? What is the role of the Holy Spirit in making plain the truths of God's Word?

Wouldn't it be great if we all could spend more time wrestling with these important questions? I've always believed that the Bible and our Christian faith can stand up to any scrutiny, but most of the time we sort of go through the motions and never really explore what Jesus sometimes called the mystery of life in the spirit. Brian and I had a great time discussing some of these issues as the countryside flew by. And what a countryside! By now it was graced with many piñon pine, attesting to a higher elevation. We marveled at the mountains around us, peaks capped by circular rows of vertical rocks, like the walls of ancient castles or the brims of royal crowns.

I sensed that essentially we had been climbing since we left the ocean. We would continue to climb until we hit the Continental Divide, then would descend until we reached the Appalachians on the East Coast. For now, though, we were able to ride and talk, and with the wind at our backs we maintained a speed of twenty-two to twenty-three miles per hour—a great, steady pace on a bike. A big part of that pace was made possible by our support van. It would be hard to imagine doing this without such a vehicle. How wonderful to be able to gulp down cold water and ice every forty-five minutes or so, or to call the van and have it deliver the big tire pump when we needed to repair a flat. Most of the time Brian and I were on our own, but it was nice to know Ted was only a cell phone call away . . . usually just around the next curve.

Small Is Beautiful

By the time we got into Truxton it was already dark—the first day we had ridden past sunset. Truxton is a tiny little town not even listed in the index at the back of my Rand McNally Road Atlas. It was established in 1951 as a stop along old Route 66 and was named for a nearby canyon and spring which had been christened by Lieutenant Edwin Beale in 1857 to honor his mother. Route 66 pumped life into the town, which in its heyday kept hopping twenty-four hours a day and supported a dozen businesses.

Truxton lies near the Colorado Plateau's edge, situated in "a broad valley covered with grasslands and forests of junipers and surrounded by a panoramic vista of hills, mesas, and cliffs with names like Music Mountain, Laughing Jack Butte, Cherokee Peak, and Cottonwood Cliffs," according to the back of a local menu, which adds, "Our valley has a history of skirmishes between the Indians and the wagon trains in the 1800s. Springs of fresh water made the long treks possible for American trailblazers. Many rugged pioneer families paused here in their journey west to let this quiet beauty ease the stress of prolonged hardships. Here they stood before the gateway of a new, untested life."

The halcyon days are long gone, however, and today Truxton offers just two motels, one of which seems defunct. The center of activity in this sleepy town ("small is beautiful, old is beautiful, slow is beautiful, safe is beautiful," says the menu) is the Frontier Cafe, a 1950s mom-and-pop business taken over in 1972 by Ray and Mildred Barker. Local legend has it that the cafe owes its existence to the supernatural. The cafe's founder, Alice Wright, supposedly inherited a large sum of money and was advised by a fortune-teller to go four hundred miles from Los Angeles and build a cafe. Frankly, I can imagine many more hospitable and picturesque spots in which an enterprising entrepreneur could establish a cafe within a four-hundred-mile radius of Los Angeles. Perhaps the legend omits the possibility that the fortune-teller owned a piece of the Arizona desert and made a quick sale to her client?

The place is still here, along with a motel and gift shop operated by Mildred and five generations of Barkers. Ray, who founded the Historic Route 66 Association, had died recently.

We stayed that night at the Barkers' Frontier Motel, a little cinder block complex of rooms immediately adjacent to the highway. We had no phone, a TV with bad reception, just a couple of electrical receptacles, an air conditioner missing its front panel so that the coils were directly exposed, and the night we stayed there—NO HOT WATER. "The repairman hasn't finished fixing it," we were told. So after a long day of riding, we were rewarded with a thirty-two dollar room that seemed more tired than we were.

But I really shouldn't complain. Although we arrived after the cafe had closed, Mildred Barker fixed us four boxed lunches and gave us our choice of beverages, reopened the cafe just for us, and allowed us to sit down at a table and eat our dinner in peace. Then when she retired for the evening, we were entertained by her ninety-year-old father-in-law.

What a delight this man was! For an hour or more he ticked off story after story about his colorful past and background, more tales than you'd find in a Sunday edition of the *Los Angeles Times*. The interesting thing was, he seldom used names. His eighty-nine-year-old wife he called "this one"; his daughter-in-law Mildred was "that one"; and his recently deceased son, Ray, was "the boy." We never did catch his own first name. Among his more memorable anecdotes:

- He was born on the Cherokee Indian reservation in the Oklahoma Territory in 1907 (he's half Indian), but moved here in 1957 because he liked the climate.
- He used to work for the U.S. military and traveled all over the country, mostly in charge of construction projects, making more money than a five-star general.
- He built the steel tower used to test the first atomic bomb near Alamogordo, New Mexico, and got to watch the blast. He said that physicist Dr. Robert Oppenheimer, the genius behind the Manhattan Project, didn't know for sure if the bomb would start a chain reaction in the atmosphere and burn up the planet, leaving it like the moon—a dead, gray, lifeless lump of sterile soil.
- He once "practically ran the state of New Mexico" and later owned a ranch that spread over three states, from New Mexico to Oklahoma to Texas. He had to pay income taxes in all three states, more than $50,000 in some years.
- He despises Federal Reserve Chairman Alan Greenspan and complained that the man is wrecking the economy. Even so, he plays around some with the stock market.
- Old Route 66 didn't decline because of the interstate, as most people think. Rather, trucks already were killing it. Instead of using railroads to ship goods across the country, as we should have, the roads were packed with truckers who drove so fast that people couldn't get back on the highway once they exited. Therefore regular people stopped getting off the highway altogether, and thus the highway died.

Despite his age and eyesight that fails beyond a distance of about three feet, this man tries to keep active. "You know," he told me, "when you're ninety you have to keep active or you just die." I've often thought the same thing, and I hope I continue to heed his advice as the years increase. In some ways, that's why I'm out on this adventure in the first place. Biking across the country when you're almost fifty is nothing like believing God's promise for a son when you're a century old (as Abraham did) or like conquering hostile territory when you're eighty-five (I think that was Caleb)—but it does take more than a small measure of faith.

Is there a big, impossible dream *you* need to embrace? I'll leave you to ponder that question as Brian and I head back to room six for a good night's sleep. Time to say good night.

When Prayer Is Like Spittin' in the Wind

The business card says, "Look for the Cowboy out front and stop at house with red tin roof." That's what visitors to Antelope Valley must do if they want to rest their weary bones awhile at Mike and Karen Landis's "Tent and Breakfast" on old Route 66, twenty miles west of Seligman, Arizona. We stopped by for lunch on Thursday, May 15, and spent a delightful couple of hours with "the better half" of the Landis household.

We didn't meet Mike because he was out working the ranch. Mike has been a cowboy all his life—not one of those dudefied, dime store frauds that laze across the screen in bad "B" movies but a real-life cowboy who makes his living by ropin', brandin', and herdin' cattle. Many of us have seen Mike but didn't realize it. For several years he has been the image featured on the greeting cards created by Leanin' Tree. He has that rugged, hardworkin' look that typifies the American cowboy. Mike is sixty-eight and just recently retired as foreman of a big local ranch. That doesn't mean he stopped working, however. In this part of the country the best paycheck a cowboy can expect to receive is about six-hundred dollars per month—and in more than five decades of life on the open range, Mike has lived through many months where the money came up far short of that. So he keeps on working.

Karen moved out to Arizona from Pennsylvania more than two decades ago when her fifteen-year-old brother lost a lung. Doctors told the family that if they wanted him to live, he needed a better climate. So the family headed to Scottsdale.

Some time later Karen moved to Seligman and started her own store, where she met her future husband. She's been married to Landis (that's what she calls him) for fifteen years; it's the second marriage for both. Karen has three children and eleven grandchildren. I asked Karen if she had much trouble with her teens. "No," she replied. "Part of the solution was no TV reception in the bunkhouse." Hmmm. Is there a lesson here?

For the last four years, Mike and Karen have operated a tent-and-breakfast business, open from April 15 to October 1. Besides a beautiful spot to camp in back of the Landis home, guests can look forward to a delicious, hearty breakfast prepared expertly by Karen as well as to a clean restroom and shower. Campers find all this by mile marker 119-1/2, four miles east of Grand Canyon Caverns. Just look to the south side of the road and pull over by the wood house with the red tin roof.

You probably couldn't tell just by looking, but there's a lot of history in that house. Not that the house itself is old—it's been standing watch over the ranch for only four years. But parts of it have logged many more miles than that. Its lumber was first part of a stagecoach stop, then later used in the spur of a train station. "And now it's our house," crows Karen, a sturdy woman with dark hair and a weathered face. She loves to describe how her home came to be.

"Seligman used to be Prescott Junction," she begins. "They made the stagecoach stop into a train stop. My husband added on to it and later we made it into a bunkhouse for single cowboys. And then when we were getting ready to leave the ranch, the owner, Mr. Campbell (who lived in Texas), he wanted it tore down because of insurance and stuff like that. So I asked him if we could have the lumber, and he said, 'Sure! That's really old lumber.' I said, 'Yeah, we figured it was close to a hundred years old. We'd like to take it and build our house out of it.' When we got done, Mr. Campbell came all the way from Texas to see it. We thought that was pretty good."

Karen admits it took a lot of work to whip that lumber into shape for a house, but neither of the Landises is afraid of a little elbow grease. The bottom boards that now grace the walls of their home were so thick with the grit of a hundred years that Karen could clean only six of them a day. One had been badly burned, so Karen sanded off the scorched section and wound up with a board of many colors, the only one of its kind in the place.

But don't think these boards are the only history to be found here. Before you can enter the Landis home, you walk over the porch, its walls festooned with elk antlers and a white-washed cattle skull, an old blue and white thermometer advertising the advantages of Packard automobiles, and a rustic plaque featuring seventeen kinds of "Bob wire." The floor of the porch boasts its own history: "We ship cattle through a place called Pica," Karen told us. "We put a lot of cattle through that place over the years. A few years back they wanted to make a new pen down there. So we asked them if we could have those old boards, and that's what the porch is made out of. We can sit out there on the swing and say, 'Well, we watched a lot of cattle driven over these boards.'"

Yet when guests drop in on Mike and Karen, their eyes won't fix on stagecoach trappings or train station implements but more likely on a sign that hangs prominently in Karen's kitchen: "May your horse never stumble, your cinch never break, your belly never grumble, your heart never ache." The sign describes hospitality, Western-style, and we benefited mightily from Karen's generous practice of it.

Over a filling meal and lively conversation, we learned a lot about the hard-yet-satisfying rhythm of life on the Arizona range. At an elevation of 5,480 feet, it takes 640 acres to support just eight cows; that's how arid it is. Yet these days it costs sixteen dollars per foot to drill a well (not including the cost of the well casing) and the water table is at 1,000 feet. The only way to make a living with those numbers is to run huge ranges, like the Landises' neighbors, the Bar 1 and the Double O's. Karen and Mike lease the small ranch they work. They raise forty-five head of cattle, enough for them and their kids. Their ranch boasts thirteen wells and thirty-three dirt basins (manmade ponds), sufficient water to keep their little herd healthy. Nobody they know has much money. So why do they stay? "We just consider it a blessing to be able to live here," Karen says simply.

To help make ends meet, Karen works at a local elderhostel and sometimes helps lead bike tours through the area.

She also sees to the tent-and-breakfast. What guests they get, they get by word of mouth; you can look till your eyes pop, but you won't spy any billboard by the side of the road or clever advertisement in the local newspaper. Why not? Because Karen believes the fun of her little business would slip away if it got too big, and "It ain't no good if the fun goes away."

And she does have fun. One day after a couple of campers had just checked in, some local dogs started yapping and making a racket. Karen had a ready solution.

"I walked up there with my husband's gun, a Colt .45, a first generation model," she said. "So I said to my campers, 'Look, I don't want to scare you, but I want to shoot them dogs because they won't shut up. Now, I'm not going to shoot the dogs, but I want to shoot in that direction. Then they'll be quiet. So I'm going to shoot this gun.' One guy looked at the gun and said, 'Wow! Can I see that gun?' I said, 'Well, let me shoot it first, two or three shots, and then you can look at it.' He says real quiet, 'You mean, it's loaded *right now?*' I said, 'You know what? If you don't have bullets in your gun, you might as well have a hammer. It's absolutely useless. So yes, it's loaded right now and I want to shoot it. Then them dogs will be quiet.' So I popped off two—Bam! Bam!—and there was a little fire off the end of the barrel. He said, 'That's really something. That's a really old gun.' I said, 'Yeah, it is. But it works.'

Something tells me that if Karen had to actually hit something with that gun, she could. I'm not real big into the handgun debate, but I don't think the antigun lobby has Karen in mind when they work to make handguns hard to get.

"The next night at about 7:30 I get a phone call," Karen told us. "This man says, 'I know that you go to bed early, but I want to stay at your tent-and-breakfast. Can you tell me how to get there?' So I told him (I'm thinking he was just up the road). Then I asked, 'Well, where are you right now?' He said, 'I'm in Flagstaff, but I could be there in a couple of hours.' I said, 'Sir, you're going to pass a whole bunch of campgrounds before you get here. You're going to pass lots of KOAs. There are a lot of places for you to stay. You don't really have to get down here; there's a lot of other places.' He said, 'Yes, I know that, but these people told me to be sure and stay at your place.'

Turns out it was the people who were up there when I shot the gun. When this guy arrived, I was showing him the campground and he says, sadly, 'We got here too late for you to shoot your gun ... didn't we?'"

And then Karen let out a long, robust, hearty laugh, just the right dessert to top off a filling lunch. It's hard to picture this woman without her ready chuckle and without a healthy sheen on her cheeks. Yet at least twice in her life—when cancer struck—the laughter slowed and her cheeks grew sallow. Still, even those difficult times were turned to good by a loving God, a God Karen loves with all her heart and serves with all her strength.

"In those days," she said, "I had been praying for the salvation of my husband for a long time. Landis saw God all around him in the sky and trees, but he didn't have him *in* him. I was praying, but I wasn't seeing anything happen because I was praying for selfish reasons—so that he could encourage *me*. When my cancer got bad the second time, I said to Landis, 'You can't help me with your prayers because God doesn't hear you. You have to have him in your heart so you can help me and the people at the church with your prayers. Otherwise, you're just spittin' in the wind.'"

He stopped spittin'. And he got saved.

These days, Karen invests a lot of her time at church. She serves as both treasurer and secretary at Calvary Baptist Church, a tiny congregation of eight couples and seventeen people in all. Tiny in numbers, but not in power. "We do a whole lot of prayin' in our church," Karen says. Not once in the last fifteen years has the church ever taken an offering, yet God always has provided. While the congregation's bills aren't astronomical—$1,000 per year to use the land, another $1,000 for taxes and electric and other utilities, plus the pastor's salary—those numbers are a stretch for this faithful congregation. Yet every year, the bills get paid. "In this little place, that we can do something like this—it's amazing," Karen exclaims.

She tells how a little while ago the church was in desperate need of a pianist when the former one moved away. In a congregation where few can carry a tune unassisted, much less play an instrument, that's a real problem. So the church started praying for a piano player. At just that time a new couple moved into the area; Karen quickly discovered the wife was an accomplished pianist. But when the lady was approached about playing for the church, she replied that she couldn't since she wasn't a Baptist. Karen convinced her to come to church just once, anyway, and that the church would be glad to pay her to play. The couple did come, they stayed, and the woman has continued to play. *Without* being paid.

"Religion to me is really a big thing, about twenty miles long," Karen explains. "God doesn't hold anyone hostage—it's a free deal."

Now the church is praying about a much bigger request— that God might send a replacement for its pastor, Warren Smith. Warren has heart trouble and is ready to retire, but he wants to stay on until a new pastor can be found. He and his church are praying very hard that someone might come to take his place, since nobody in the area is able to replace him. Karen is right in the middle of those prayers. And she promises, "We take care of the pastor good. We're small, but we're mighty. We've seen God work here like you wouldn't believe. Like in overtime. He's taken care of us in overtime."

By the time we had to leave the Landis homestead at a little past noon, Karen had extracted a promise from us to join her church in prayer for a new pastor. She wouldn't take any money to cover the cost of the meal; what she wanted was our prayers. We gladly agreed and gratefully said our good-byes.

Everywhere we went, we found people like that. It's the old glass half-empty/half-full story. Karen looks at life as half full and finds ways to fill the rest of it. Sometimes I think the rest of us fail to realize how full our glasses really are. When I hear of all the problems many of our families are having, I think of Karen and Mike's simple life. Have we accumulated too much stuff to enjoy the simple pleasures? Can we find ways to return to a simpler way of life without moving to the desert?

Family Ties

The unincorporated town of Ash Fork lies at an elevation of 5,142 feet, while we began the day in Truxton at about 4,300 feet. Do the math and you can see that my theory about heading uphill to the Continental Divide held true. At least we didn't have to climb the summits in front of us. Kaibab and Coconino National Forest mountain peaks dominated our eastern horizon. Bill Williams Mountain (9,256 feet) and Humphrey's Peak (at 12,611 feet, the highest point in Arizona) stood gleaming in the distance. Still, the climb up Ash Fork gave us reason to perspire; while the average May temperature here is seventy-eight degrees, on this day it reached ninety-two. And that's tough on any body, whether it be made of flesh or of steel.

The latter observation was proven true when we encountered a disabled van partway up the Ash Fork hill. An elderly gentleman on his way to Illinois lurched to a stop when his van's top radiator hose burst. We diagnosed the problem, he cut the hose and reconstructed it, poured in two gallons of fresh water (which he was carrying), and later passed us with a friendly honk.

He and his wife had lived in Illinois from the '40s through the '70s. Before moving to California, they purchased ten acres of land with energetic plans to build a new home in Illinois when retirement rolled around. Last year they built their brick dream house . . . only to change their minds about moving back to the Midwest. All their children have settled in California and the tug of family ties became too great to resist. He was heading to Illinois to check out his never-lived-in home, then planned to return to California for the marriage of one grandson and the birthday of another.

"As much as we loved the house, we love the kids and their kids more," he said. "I just hope we can sell the house and not lose too much. The market's not very good where we built."

I don't rejoice that this man and his wife spent so many of their resources building a home they'll never use, but I confess it does my heart good to meet someone to whom family ties are much stronger than the lure of material possessions. It doesn't happen enough in our society.

During a recent "in studio" conversation at *Focus on the Family*, former U.S. Secretary of Education William Bennett shared with Dr. James Dobson and me an experience he had while away on a business trip. Bill lives in Virginia and had been speaking on the other side of the country. He was scheduled to fly back home, but in just two days he was to fly back to the West Coast for a meeting with several key executives— perhaps it would be best if he simply stayed where he was rather than making a trip home for thirty-six hours and crossing the nation twice.

He placed a call to his house to discuss the idea with his wife. His then four-year-old son answered the phone and Bill quickly asked him how he was. "Fine," came the reply. Bill then asked him about preschool and the exchange continued for several minutes until Bill finally asked, "Well, is your mother there, and can I talk with her?" When his son answered, "Yes, who may I say is calling?" Bill knew he would be going home. The thought that his own son didn't recognize his voice told him his work and travel schedule had badly intruded upon his proper priorities!

Of course, something like that could never happen in *your* home, right?

The terrain around Williams is much different from that of Arizona's West Coast or Central Territory, the areas we had just ridden through. Williams calls itself the "Gateway to the Grand Canyon[(R)]" for good reason. The city sits only fifty-nine miles from the South Rim of the canyon, the shortest route to the most heavily touristed part of one of the world's seven natural wonders. At an elevation of 6,770 feet, Williams offers cool temperatures and gorgeous vistas. For the first time on our trip, we could see snow-capped mountains in the near distance.

Williams also provides the headquarters for Kaibab National Forest. The town is named after a nineteenth-century trapper named William Sherley Williams who was born in Rutherford County, North Carolina, in 1787. "Old Bill" became a roving Baptist preacher and lived near or among the Osage Indians for many years. As early as 1826 he joined a trapping party in Arizona, and for the rest of his life he ranged at will from Oregon to Old Mexico. "Schooled in the ways of the Indian," Old Bill was "a successful and astute trapper, a clever and cool-headed man in battle, and one who knew how to handle his rifle in a fight."[1] Some historians consider him the greatest of all mountain men. It is believed he was killed by Ute Indian warriors in southern Colorado on March 14, 1849. Today an eight-and-a-half-foot, one-thousand-pound bronze statue honoring the old trapper/preacher stands in Monument Park at the west end of town.

Our accommodations at the British-owned El Rancho Motel were graciously provided for us by members of the Canyon Chapel Four Square Church. Sarah and Dennis Massey, old friends from Burbank, California, also put together a church dinner for us. The Masseys and Nancy and I had been members of the same age-graded Sunday school class. As far as I knew, Dennis always had been in the funeral business, but now he was obviously more concerned about the living than the dead. I learned that night that Dennis was about to be ordained as an Episcopal priest. As we departed the church, he said to me, "I'm anxious to be a conservative, evangelical influence within the Episcopal Church. I know it won't be easy, but I feel God has called me to it."

Time and again we spoke with people who understood who they were in God's eyes. Perhaps on the back roads, in the smaller towns, it's easier to sort out God's call from the other screaming voices we hear each day. Peggy Benson, the widow of the late author and speaker Bob Benson, describes the process as "listening to a God who whispers."

I was interested in a rare document the Williams congregation has hanging in its lobby, a church charter signed in 1940 by Aimee Semple McPherson. Aimee founded the International Church of the Foursquare Gospel in 1926, and although some controversy still surrounds her life and career,[2] the Foursquare church she left behind has thrived. Many of its congregations have excelled at evangelism. The Williams church has spawned a number of sister congregations in the area and undoubtedly has played a key role in the community.

We greatly appreciated the dinner the church provided for us and were interested to hear of an intriguing thread woven through the previous two days of our journey. In Needles, Ed and Linda Davenport told us of a cycling group which had stayed at their Super 8 motel. A young girl with multiple sclerosis, part of the team, suffered from a deformed foot. Ed prayed for the girl and described seeing her foot healed! Now we heard that this very team had come through Williams and also were at a dinner provided by the Foursquare church. Small world!

Wherever people gather, someone always has the gift of hospitality. This is not unique to Christians, but it is a certainty within the church. As we traveled across the nation, kindness, hospitality, and generosity were our constant companions, embodied in the lives of the people we met. The heart of America is a generous heart, and we benefited from that generosity more times than we could count.

The stretch of highway from Flagstaff to Tuba City is said to be among the deadliest roads in America—and the visual evidence confirms the claim. Everywhere we looked there seemed to be crosses marking the spot of someone's death. Wooden crosses. Plastic crosses. Crosses hung with wreaths. Crosses decorated with rosary beads. Crosses commemorating the name and date of death of a loved one. Crosses everywhere, each one of them, I'm sure, soaked in tears.

In fact, only two other states can rival Arizona for yearly bicycle fatalities (Louisiana and Florida are the other two). And this chunk of highway in what is called Indian Country is among the most lethal in the state.

Moving toward Tuba City, Brian and I entered the Navajo Indian reservation and passed what appeared to be a dead man lying in the ditch. Brian was the only one to see him and said, "Did you see that?" I responded, "What?" Brian burst out, "There's a dead Indian back there!" I thought it couldn't be and rode on in silence. After several seconds Brian asked, "Well, aren't we going back?" More than a little concerned about what we would find I reluctantly reversed direction and retraced our tracks.

By the time we returned it became clear that we were not going to be dealing with a dead man because he was sitting up. We had met enough Native Americans to see that he was most likely Navajo. He had been face down in the sand, but now he was groggily brushing himself off. We stopped and asked if he was OK.

"Yeah. Yeah, I'm OK," he replied, shakily. Several empty bottles surrounded him. In these parts people walk everywhere, and he'd obviously been walking and drinking and just passed out in the hot sun, falling in the ditch.

There wasn't much we could do for him on bicycles. And while he did want a ride, he didn't know quite where. "I need to go . . . I need to go . . . *there*," he said with a wave of his hand in a vague northerly direction. The predicament seemed a normal part of life for him, certainly nothing unusual. At last we said good-bye and resumed our journey toward Tuba City, praying that someone would provide transportation for our inebriated friend.

According to the *American Indian Digest* (1995 edition), alcoholism affects seventy-five percent of Native American homes; Fetal Alcohol Syndrome is thirty-three times higher among Indians than among non-Indians; and alcoholic mortality is ten times the rate of all other ethnic groups combined. Navajos have the largest reservation and tribe and live with some of the most difficult conditions. Forty-six percent have no electricity; fifty-four percent have no indoor plumbing; eighty-two percent live without a telephone. These Third World living conditions are typical of most reservation communities, and frankly, it is very troubling to me. The story of our country's first inhabitants is a sad one, and I am grateful for the few Christian ministries that are working with these wonderful people. We do not need to look very far to find a mission field.

This incident reminded me of our encounter with Rodney Jones the day before. I felt helpless on both occasions. Just as with Rodney, we barely touched the outermost edge of this Navajo's life. I wanted to do more. He needed to know that satisfaction could never be found in a bottle, that this is a wonderful land of opportunity where doors swing wide for those with initiative and a solid work ethic. If a soapbox had been close by, I probably would have climbed up and begun to address my audience like the keynote speaker at an Amway rally. But there was only the bike, the road, and the sand. And so I prayed.

Lord, bring someone into this man's life who will introduce him to you, and may our concern be helpful in his journey. Amen.

Soon the phone in the van was ringing, and I knew it was time for another interview with Dr. Dobson.

Interview Two

Dobson: Hello, Michael! . . . It is Friday afternoon as we speak. Where in the world are you?

Trout: I'm on Highway 89 north of Flagstaff, Arizona, headed toward Tuba City out on the Navajo reservation. We plan on staying there tonight.

Dobson: Tuba City?

Trout: Tuba City.

Dobson: That's not one of the big metropolises, is it?

Trout: No, we haven't been staying in *any* of the big metropolises.

Dobson: You made it through the desert, Mike!

Trout: Oh, we did. They had an unusually hot spell and for several days it was up over 110. And I think out on the pavement it was probably 130.

Dobson: Unbelievable!

Trout: It really was warm and we drank three or four gallons of water a day per person.

Dobson: Now, I also heard that you've been doing some climbing.

Trout: We have. Coming out of Needles if you take old Route 66, there is an incredible hill that is very tough to climb on a bike. And then yesterday, going from Ash Fork, Arizona, to Williams, Arizona, there is what they call the Ash Fork Hill, where you climb almost 2,500 feet in about fifteen miles. That's probably the longest, steepest hill we've had. You know, Doctor, we have found that the late afternoon and evening is a better time for us. And we did that climb in the late afternoon. We just have more energy then, so I'm glad we hit it when we did.

Dobson: Are those trucks going by that I hear behind you?

Trout: They are. This is not a very safe road. There's no shoulder on the road; you're just pedaling along the highway with everyone else. And I'm kind of glad to take a break right at this moment.

Dobson: Mike, tell me about the friends that are coming out to greet you. Anybody saying hello as you go by?

Trout: Oh, they sure are. As a matter of fact, we just stopped riding with a couple of men who wanted to join up with us in Flagstaff and then ride part of the way out to Tuba City. One man was a locksmith and he'd heard about the ride on the broadcast. The other is a music minister at a church in Flagstaff. Both of them rode with us for probably fifteen miles. And then we had the van take them back, which I think they were happy for. It was a dangerous stretch of road. We had dinner last night in Williams, Arizona. A Foursquare church prepared the meal and had quite a group for us to spend time with. We had just a wonderful time. We also stayed with a Christian couple in Needles who own a motel. We had some great conversation with them. They love *Focus on the Family.*

Dobson: Mike, this will be heard on Tuesday. We're talking on Friday afternoon, May 16. Where will you be at the time this is heard?

Trout: Let's see. On Tuesday we'll be in Colorado, crossing the bottom of the state. We will have gone up over Wolf Creek Pass and we'll be heading down on the eastern side of the Rockies by then. And hopefully we'll have a number of folks come down from Colorado Springs to join us for a few hours.

Dobson: You're getting close to home, but you're really not stopping. You're heading on to the East Coast.

Trout: We sure are. Someone asked me earlier today what the Lord has been saying to me out here. I think probably the most vivid thing so far is that prayers are answered. A lot of people have been praying for us. We have had plenty of opportunities for trouble, but we have had no difficulties. We've stayed on schedule, and I know that's because of answered prayer.

Dobson: Well, it's always fun getting an update from you, Mike.

Trout: Hey, thank you! It's quite an adventure. It's everything I thought it would be and much, much more.

Dobson: Blessings to you, and stay in touch with us!

Navajoland is like nowhere else on earth. The territory of the Navajo nation covers more than 27,000 square miles of astonishing beauty, extending into the states of Arizona, Utah, and New Mexico—larger than the entire state of West Virginia. The reservation, the largest in the country, is home to twelve lakes and ponds and encompasses more than a dozen national monuments, tribal parks, and historical sites. Stunning mountain ranges, vast sage-covered valleys, and enchanting wind-carved canyons combine to form a landscape unparalleled anywhere on the planet.

Yet as lovely as this countryside appears during the day, its beauty intensifies as dusk approaches. The red Moenkopi sandstone seems to deepen in color even as the contrasting limestone brightens. Wild and majestic rock shapes formed by wind and water and volcanic activity, silhouetted by the setting sun, suggest a massive landlocked ship here or a heaven-reaching church there.

The views simply overwhelmed me. I envisioned myself landing on another planet, looking out a portal and taking in this terrain. In my report back to mission control I would say, "There's no life that I can see, and yet somebody's missing a marvelous opportunity to live somewhere beautiful. There's a pristine beauty here that takes away your breath. Civilization has left no scars."

The Navajo who populate this land now number almost 200,000. They call themselves the *Diné* and strive hard to blend traditional and modern ways of living. Scores of roadside stands offer traditional Navajo crafts, especially silver jewelry adorned with turquoise, beautiful rugs woven with many variations of traditional designs, and ceremonial baskets.

And I will always remember Navajoland for one further gift of beauty: a stiff wind at our backs. To a bicyclist, almost nothing is more intoxicating.

Some Public Schools Really Work!

We stole into Tuba City just before darkness fell. Somehow, almost every city from Williams to Tuba City seemed farther away than it was supposed to be. The mileage posted on all the road signs was just a little off and the road itself was tougher than we had anticipated. To top it off, we had a horrible time trying to find accommodations. The area is jammed with tour buses bound for the Grand Canyon, and motel rooms are at a premium. Canyon Country is heavily promoted around the world and it seems to be paying off; every time we stopped to eat we noticed patrons who spoke languages other than English. Of course, these folks had reservations; we didn't. The Quality Inn did have one room with two beds for $105, but we said no thanks.

After scouring the town, eventually we found Greyhills Inn, a motel/hostel run by Navajo high school students. Their rooms cost a paltry $47.52, double occupancy. Located at the south entrance of Greyhills Academy High School, home of the Tuba City High Warriors, Greyhills Inn looks and functions like a dormitory. It's part of a program to train students for post-graduation employment in the hospitality industry.

"Anywhere from seventeen to twenty-four students have been enrolled in our semester-long hospitality class," the manager of the program told us. "Students train for all roles in motel services, from maintenance to housekeeping to bookkeeping. Our program has been operating for seven years and has earned a good track record."

And what is this motel/hostel like? Think of a college dorm room, only slightly larger, and you have a good picture of any of the thirty-two rooms at Greyhills Inn. Rooms come equipped with telephone jacks, but no telephones. There's a TV, a couple of double beds, a lamp, a few pictures hanging on the wall, and that's it. Bathrooms are dormitory style with community showers. A sign on the Coke-dispensing machine in the lobby warns, "Motel will NOT be liable for injuries resulting in tilting and shaking of machine." Another sign above the check-in counter tells patrons that public showers are available Sunday through Saturday from 11:00 A.M. to 6:00 P.M. for two dollars per person, regardless of age. And of course, "Provide your own towel, washcloth, soap, shampoo, etc."

We hear a lot about the sad state of public education in this country, but I've got to tell you—this was very impressive. This school was preparing its students for the real world. They were learning more than the motel business. They were learning personal responsibility. Even those students who will never manage a motel or hotel will know how to run a business. I think a lot of high schools in America should introduce similar programs.

By the time we finished our dinner it was after 10:00 P.M., but despite the late hour, Brian and I visited a Tuba City laundromat. The place must have had a hundred washers and almost that many dryers. Every machine looked well used; thousands of hands had gone in and out of those machines, wearing off the paint (but not destroying the reliability) of all those Maytag wonders.

While we waited for the clothes to finish, we sat out in the van, looked across the desert, and chatted. Dilapidated houses were down the road, and a busy McDonald's restaurant was across the street. I pondered the poor surroundings and thought, *As the Manifest Destiny marched west, civilization took over and created a scar on the land in many places where once there had been beauty.* But I also pondered the hopelessness that seemed to permeate this region. After four centuries of active missionary effort, less than eight percent of the native population are born-again Christians. On some reservations, the figure is under 1 percent. Despite the stark beauty of this part of Arizona, I felt a profound sadness for the people. When you study Native American history over the last four hundred years, there is little that brings joy to your soul. Bemoaning all the injustices Indian people have suffered at the hands of the European immigrants, an older Native American man quipped, "We should have had stricter immigration laws." Despite the smile that comment may prompt, it does not cover the fact that we have forgotten Paul's metaphor in 1 Corinthians 12 where he equates the church with the human body. He warns us against acting as though one part is more important than another. We are of equal worth and value, and we desperately need each other for complete health.

After a good night's sleep, it was time to leave. I got out the bike stand to clean up our cycles, oiled their chains, and fixed my rear tire, then all of us headed to Katy's Cafe for the breakfast special (two eggs, two pieces of bacon, two pancakes, $2.95). By now it was mid morning, and we were on the road once again.

As difficult as the ride had been the day before, the eighth day of our adventure provided our best riding to date. A tail-wind most of the day enabled us to move at an average of twenty-five to twenty-six miles per hour, sometimes more than thirty mph. The shoulder was adequate although etched with deep grooves running perpendicular to the road. These are designed to awaken drivers who fall asleep at the wheel; when their tires drift across the grooves, it's like trying to fall asleep next to an obnoxious alarm clock. Great for cars, but tough for bicycles. To avoid them we had to ride either outside them next to the dirt or inside them next to the road. And if you're cruising along at twenty-five to twenty-seven mph on the outside edge with just six to eight inches of pavement between you and the dirt, there's not a lot of room for error. If a gust of wind catches you and makes you swerve onto the soft ground, you go down. And not gracefully. Fortunately, we never found out how well the soft ground cushions a fall.

We stopped for a late lunch at the Anasazi Inn, where I tried the Navajo Fry Bread with Beef—a huge sandwich half the size of a platter. You say you've never tried Navajo Fry Bread? Then I suggest you give it a shot.

Navajo Fry Bread

2 cups unsifted flour
1/2 cup dry milk solids
2 teaspoons double-acting baking powder
1/2 teaspoon salt
2 tablespoons lard, cut into 1/2-inch bits, plus 1 pound
    lard for deep frying
1/2 cup ice water

Combine the flour, dry milk solids, baking power, and salt, and sift them into a deep bowl. Add the 2 tablespoons of lard bits and, with your fingertips, rub the flour and fat together until the dough can be gathered into a ball. Drape the bowl with a kitchen towel and let the dough rest at room temperature for about two hours.

After the resting period, cut the dough into three equal pieces. Then, on a lightly floured surface, roll each piece into a rough circle about 8 inches in diameter and 1/4-inch thick. With a small, sharp knife, cut two 4- to 5-

inch-long parallel slits completely through the dough down the center of each round, spacing the slits about 1 inch apart.

In a heavy 10-inch skillet, melt the remaining pound of lard over moderate heat until it is very hot but not smoking. The melted fat should be about 1 inch deep; add more lard if necessary. Fry the breads one at a time for about 2 minutes on each side, turning them once with tongs or a slotted spatula. The bread will puff slightly and become crisp and brown. Drain the Navajo fry bread on paper towels and serve warm.

Makes three 8-inch round breads.

Then ride forty miles to work off the fat, which we did, out to mile marker 421. Having passed no other accommodations we loaded the bikes in the van and headed back to the Anasazi Inn for the night. With a total of 102 miles logged for the day, we thought we'd earned another piece of Navajo Fry Bread.

Just Serving the Lord

Between Mexican Water and Red Mesa we passed a billboard advertising the Solid Rock Outreach Center, sponsors of a "Miracle Revival" featuring Pastor Don Aime from Scottsdale, Arizona, and the Rev. Mona Taylor, June 2–14 at 7:00 P.M. If readers needed "Salvation Healing Deliverance," this was the place for them. Brian and I stopped to look around and noted there wasn't a lodging for as far as the eye could see. Who in the world were they going to minister to out here?

Later we heard that a crowd of hundreds—yea, thousands—was anticipated. Brian and I didn't stop in, but Ted and Steve wandered back to the complex to learn more. Two miles back from the highway, on a dirt road, under the watchful eyes of horses grazing in fields nearby, they found the church, the Solid Rock Power Miracle Living Crusade, led by Pastor Clarence Dee. The small church meets in a cement block building while a new facility is under construction to the west. Two green outhouses stand next to that, marked in black letters outlined in white, GIRLS or BOYS.

Pastor Dee wasn't home, but his daughter-in-law Tina was. "This is my husband's home church," Tina explained.

"The ministry has been around a long time." She told us their biggest outreach was the tent meeting to be held the first week in August, at which thousands of people were expected in response to some planned radio advertisements. She repeatedly invited all of us to return if we were in the area at that time. Tina herself travels and performs with Christian bands around the area. "We're just serving the Lord," she said.

We're just serving the Lord. I wonder what would happen if everyone who names the name of Christ could honestly say the same thing? Way out here in Navajoland, Tina Dee and her family are "just serving the Lord," and people who never before knew the God of the universe are being introduced to him and are being grafted into his ever-blessed family.

It doesn't take much to "just serve the Lord." You don't have to be rich. You don't have to be famous. You don't have to preach to millions or discover a cure for cancer or build a vast television ministry or do any number of things we sometimes mistakenly think we need to do to "just serve the Lord." All we have to do is be faithful where we are, right now. Whatever gifts and abilities and resources we have we can use to serve God. As the apostle Paul says, "We have different gifts, according to the grace given us. If a man's gift is prophesying, let him use it in proportion to his faith. If it is serving, let him serve; if it is teaching, let him teach; if it is encouraging, let him encourage; if it is contributing to the needs of others, let him give generously; if it is leadership, let him govern diligently; if it is showing mercy, let him do it cheerfully" (Rom. 12:6–8).

I'm glad that there are many dedicated believers who feel especially called to this part of the country and to lead these people to Christ. They're in the absolute middle of nowhere; yet here they are, a little church planning a big revival in just a few weeks. We could all use a dose of that huge faith.

In my role as cohost on the *Focus on the Family* radio program, my service is more visible than that of some others. But I didn't seek the opportunity; it was simply another open door in a series of service commitments. I discovered long ago that if we are available for God's use, he will lead us to opportunities to serve him with the special gifts he gave us.

The marvelous evidence of being in God's service is that you can look back over your life and see how each step was divinely used to prepare you. Sometimes the path is a little uncomfortable and it feels like you are running barefoot over hot sand. But most of us know through personal experience that the soul toughens and what once seemed impossible becomes bearable. That's when you grow more effective and often are ready for a bigger challenge.

What are you good at? Whatever it is, find a way to use it in the service of the King. Because, of course, there really is no such thing as "just" serving the Lord. For when you serve the King, whatever form your service takes, you are involved in heavenly, eternal business—business that he sees and notices and is determined to reward. This is so important to him that he even closes his book with it: "Behold, I am coming soon! My reward is with me, and I will give to everyone according to what he has done" (Rev. 22:12).

And no "just" about it.

Quick Trip Through Four States

Four Corners Monument is the only place in the United States where four states meet. Visitors can stand on a single piece of real estate and simultaneously inhabit Arizona, New Mexico, Utah, and Colorado. The monument was surveyed and established by the U.S. government several times, beginning in 1868. The current marker is made of granite, a bronze disk, and colored concrete, and includes embedded metal plates of the great seal from each of the four states. An inscription at the site reads, "Four States Here Meet In Freedom Under God."

After taking the obligatory photo (many visitors insist on placing one hand or foot on a corner of each state, spread-eagle fashion, and snapping a picture in that undignified pose, but we shunned such a shot and settled for a more upright position), we briefly toured the many gift stands and then had lunch.

While eating we met the family of Oliver Wang, a businessman from Taipei, Taiwan. The Wangs were on vacation in the midst of a two-month tour of the United States. Five years ago the Wangs took a similar trip, and now that their daughter was sixteen, they thought it would be fun to repeat the experience.

Oliver wanted to know where and why we were biking and almost immediately reached for his wallet to make a donation to our trip. I refused his kind offer, but suggested that the charity for which Brian was raising money, Kids Across America, would be a good substitute. He promptly handed Brian a $50 bill, the first cash donation he had received since leaving California.

We gave a T-shirt to each of the Wang family (father, mother, daughter, and son), and Oliver's daughter instantly tried hers on. We pulled out the camera and snapped several photos to remember the moment. As we rotated photographers and cameras so that everyone could get a picture, I felt the world grow a little smaller. People from two different cultures and distinct parts of this planet had come together in common excitement for a few precious moments. This, too, was a piece of the heart of America—a land where a family from Taiwan can travel openly, without border guards at every state line. Where freedom is the order of the day, not fear.

We thanked Oliver for his generous gift once more, then sat down to finish eating. In moments Oliver's son approached us and, without speaking a word (apparently Oliver was the only one in his family who speaks English), offered us a package of Miss Kate's Coffee Cream biscuits, made in Singapore. And once more we were the beneficiaries of the Wang family's generosity.

As we left the Four Corners Monument, straining up a steep hill, the Wang vehicle sped past with windows rolled down, the family shouting their good-byes and well wishes. We waved good-bye to them and Arizona and strained toward Colorado ... and our meeting with the Wolf.

CHAPTER 4

Staring Down the Wolf

In midafternoon of May 18, we crossed the San Juan River and were greeted by a sign that promised "Mountains and a whole lot more." The sign could mean only one thing: We had arrived in Colorado!

As we pushed into Cortez, a beige pickup truck passed us slowly, then turned around and pulled up alongside. Len Goebel, a contractor from Durango, got out and greeted us. "I've been out in California," he said, "and heard about your trip on the radio. I figured this was the way you'd go and I've been looking for you the last two days." Len offered us a place to stay and to eat and said, "However we can help, you just let us know." Before he left he handed us his business card and said wistfully, "I'm glad you're doing this. I wish I could join you."

Len's last comment was anything but unusual. We must have heard such a wish longingly expressed at least two dozen times over the course of our adventure, but always followed by reasons why they could never attempt such a thing as our "wild" adventure. But why? Why do so many of us trudge along in a rut? Do we honestly think that adventure is best left to kids, something we have to give up when we hit thirty?

I would never promote irresponsibility or reckless disregard for life, but how would it really hurt you to try something out of the ordinary? I'll never forget the challenge given by Tim Hansel, author and adventurer, to a group of men gathered for a church retreat. Tim used a round tabletop to illustrate most of our lives. He placed a piece of chalk in the center of the circle and said, "This is where most of you live. You're safe and comfortable, while opportunities and adventures circle by out here," motioning toward the edge. "All of you need to stretch, to move outside of your comfort zone and experience life more fully. If you do, God will use you in ways you've never imagined."

It was Tim who first took me mountain climbing and rappelling. He taught me how to depend on others and on God in a way I'd never known. As a result, I accomplished things I'd only imagined . . . like backing off a one-hundred foot precipice and descending, with faith in my belay line and the belayer at the top. I moved from the center to the edge very quickly.

When we venture into the unknown—however exotic or mundane it may appear to others—we leave our comfort zones behind and invite God to lead us to new heights of spiritual maturity. We learn secrets about ourselves, both pleasant and distressing, that we might never have discovered in any other setting. Godly adventure opens up vast panoramas of possibility for spiritual and human growth. Sure, it can be frightening, but that makes the thrill all the more delectable.

The Pueblo People

The Mesa Verde Plateau provides visitors with spectacular vistas no matter where they look. From Park Point, at 8,571 feet, you can see more than one hundred miles into Colorado, Arizona, New Mexico, and Utah. Fauna is plentiful in the area, with mountain lions, bobcats, deer, mountain sheep, elk, eagles, hawks, and other raptors each staking out their territory. Local plant life is a unique blend of species found in mountains and deserts.

It was here, in this dazzling countryside, that a mysterious people called the Anasazi carved out a Stone Age living for more than a thousand years.

Mesa Verde (Spanish for "green table") was the first U.S. national park set aside for the "preservation . . . of the sites and the other works and relics of prehistoric man." It was established by Congress on June 29, 1906. Here a fascinating and mysterious civilization was carved into the cliffs and valleys of the Colorado Plateau, between the majestic San Juan Mountains and the Sonoran Desert. All-year-round visitors can walk through cliff dwellings and numerous mesa-top villages built by a little-known ancestral Pueblo people between A.D. 600 and A.D. 1300. For good reason it is one of the most popular attractions in the Southwest.

The vanished people the Navajo call the Anasazi, or "Ancient Ones," first settled the region about the time of Christ. They were hunters, traders, artisans, and farmers, and this was the heart of their civilization for more than a millennium.

Yet despite decades of archeological work—the first modern exploration of the cliff dwellings began a century ago—much is still unknown about the Anasazi of Mesa Verde. Since no written records exist, what is known of their impressive civilization must be inferred from the ruins and even the trash they left behind. The Anasazi tossed their refuse down the slopes in front of their homes, and from these garbage heaps, filled with scraps of food, broken pottery, tools, and other unwanted refuse, come sketchy insights into their daily lives.

Have you ever thought about the things people could learn about you if they studied your garbage?

Today, visitors can walk through five major cliff dwellings and numerous mesa-top villages built by the Anasazi, the mysterious people who were "so skillful at wresting a living from a difficult land," in the words of a tourism brochure.

For Brian and me, however, the mystery would have to remain for a while longer. More than anything else, we needed a good meal and a firm bed. We'd find both in the quaint little town of Mancos. We had intended to bike to Durango on this day, but instead wound up staying in Mancos (elevation 6,993) at the Enchanted Mesa Motel. If I didn't live in Colorado Springs and didn't work for Focus on the Family, I could see myself settling down in such a lovely old town. Mancos is a quiet village nestled in a beautiful valley between the La Plata mountains and Mesa Verde National Park. After a long and tiring ride, it offered the perfect combination of natural beauty and homespun hospitality.

Ranchers settled the Mancos River Valley in the 1880s, among them some Quakers from Pennsylvania named the

Wetherills. The Wetherills ranched in the southern part of Mancos Valley and were the first white men to extensively explore the cliff dwellings of Mesa Verde. A little over a century ago in 1891 the Rio Grande Southern Railroad reached Mancos on its way to the silver mines of Telluride and Rico. The little town boomed, becoming a thriving commercial center with an economy based on lumber, cattle, and the produce grown in Montezuma Valley to the west. Things have settled down some since then, but it was here, in the parking lot of the motel, that we enjoyed one of the best conversations of our trip.

Doy and MaryAnn Graf are hay farmers, partners in the business with Doy's brother. They saw us loading our bikes into the van outside of Mesa Verde and decided to track us down. There are only two motels in Mancos, so they didn't have to search long. They were eager to say "thank you" to *Focus on the Family* because of all the radio program has meant to them, especially in the last year and half. Why the last eighteen months? Neither was sure, but both said they became more involved with the broadcast in that time. And what about their family?

"We have two teenage sons," Doy said. To which Mary-Ann quickly added, "and we worry about them a lot. They're good boys, but this world has a powerful pull on kids these days away from God." The boys are fifteen and eighteen and Doy asked the same question I've heard repeatedly at *Focus on the Family:* "Does being a parent get any easier after the teenage years?"

Reading between the lines, I suspected they had their hands full, but I assured them there was light at the end of the tunnel. The teenage years are often difficult and there's no use in trying to deny the fact. Yet in my experience with the broadcast and in my own life as the father of three girls, two of whom are now in their twenties, I can honestly say that disaster is not nearly so likely as it sometimes feels.

A case in point occurred just recently. A young mom of three daughters attended Nancy's Bible study group, and Nancy learned that she and her husband were going through some difficulties. She dropped out of the study and Nancy and I lost track of the family. But she wove back into our life when

I started visiting the gym regularly in preparation for the bike trip. She played racquetball and I would watch the games just to occupy my time as I worked on the stationary bike. She would say hello and we'd catch up on each other and at least be aware that we were all still alive.

Then one day she called Nancy and began to tell her that things had deteriorated badly in her life. She had had an affair but was trying to turn things around. Whatever Nancy said to her must have helped, because the woman sent her several marvelous thank-you notes in gratitude for all of her help. Then one day Nancy invited Rebekah, our oldest daughter, to join her for lunch with this young woman. Rebekah had seen her share of tough times, and Nancy thought she might have some real insights to share with this troubled woman. Boy, were her instincts right!

"I almost cried through the whole lunch," Nancy told me, "because I sat back and I watched Rebekah counsel, console, challenge, and comfort this woman out of her own experiences. Right before me I saw the wonderful, Christian, mature woman we always wanted her to be. And, in fact, that is exactly what she has become!" Despite our worries, those things that she was taught when she was younger never left. They were there all the time; they were simply covered over by rebellion and peer pressure and whatever else suppressed them for a time. But at some point, they all bubbled back to the surface.

Time and again I have seen at work the wisdom of the famous verse in Proverbs: "Train a child in the way he should go, and when he is old he will not turn from it" (22:6).

That verse is often misunderstood as a promise that wayward children will certainly return to the faith after sowing their youthful wild oats, but that's not what it teaches at all. It's a proverb, *not* a promise, and what it declares is that godly parenting usually results in godly children. That is, if we train our children in the way they should go—living in the fear of the Lord, for the glory of God and for the blessing of others, and according to their unique bents and talents—then, no matter how dismal some period of adolescence may appear, it is far more likely that our children will turn out to be God-fearing, healthy, productive members of society. That's the way life usually works under God's heaven, and that should give all of us great hope and encouragement.

As in everything else, our job is to be faithful stewards of what God has given to us (including our kids); God's job is to work "for the good of those who love him, who have been called according to his purpose" (Rom. 8:28). And that's where we must ultimately leave the question, "Does it get any better?"

The Grafs are also concerned about this nation, the country they love, and were quick to say they believe its people are a lot better than the news media or Hollywood would lead us to believe. Their comments fit exactly with my own conviction. Most of our news comes out of four places: New York, Los Angeles, Chicago, and Washington, D.C. I'm convinced that tends to skew our view of the world, sometimes badly. Most of America is simply not like New York or Washington or Los Angeles or Chicago. Who wouldn't get a jaundiced view of our nation by constantly peering at it through smog-colored glasses?

My trip through the heart of America convinced me I'm right about this. I certainly conducted no scientifically rigorous survey, but in state after state and city after city, I found scores of people like the Grafs who pay their taxes and support local law enforcement officials and pray for their kids and help out their neighbors and are active in church and haven't yet stuffed their homes with enough munitions to blow up a small country. And I'm not the only one to see this.

David Lamb, in his book *Over the Hills: A Midlife Escape Across America by Bicycle,* observed, "I was struck by how great is the divide between rural and urban America. Our big coastal population centers may set the national agenda, but the quiet voices I heard along forgotten routes carried, I thought, an important message. They were the voices of the other America—an America that is old-fashioned, hardworking, trusting, decent—and if we who live in the cities listened to them more attentively, we would feel better about the country, and ourselves."[1]

America is not yet beyond hope largely because of solid citizens like the Grafs who wonder what they can do to help improve the moral climate of this great nation. This is still a grassroots country, and we must never forget that!

So what can we do to make a difference? The Grafs and I talked a lot about getting involved wherever God has placed us, about helping to meet whatever needs might exist right in our own communities.

I think of Dan Panetti of the Dallas Association for Decency and his group's letter-writing campaign. They successfully removed a top-rated radio talk show from the Dallas airwaves simply by contacting the show's advertisers and reporting the specifics of the host's on-air, sex-laden antics.

I remember Tom Andes, a high school student in Northeast Ohio who decided that teachers, administrators, and students praying around the flagpole one day a year wasn't enough. He thought prayer was needed every day, so he began as a lonely prayer warrior of one. Soon another joined him, then another. By the time the school year ended, his idea had spread to four other campuses and more than 150 students were praying daily.

And I think of Doctors Grey Thomas and Jay Jamieson, who successfully convinced the Keizer, Oregon, school board task force that a school-based health clinic was a bad idea. But they didn't stop there—they then organized a local physician referral network for the district so that students who had legitimate needs had a place to turn.

These people and so many others we met across the country are just like the Grafs, people who care deeply about their families and communities and churches. In fact, on that Sunday night, the Grafs had just returned from their evening church service. Doy said he had spoken up in the service—I am not sure about what—but I suppose he voiced some prayer requests at the end of the service, as is often done in smaller congregations at the end of a Sunday evening program. It's earnest prayers like that which can make a real, eternal difference—especially when they're followed up with appropriate action!

"Shifty" Is Getting Stronger!

Ted had warned us that two formidable hills separated us from Durango. The first was Mancos Hill, just outside of town, a challenge at more than five miles of a steady four to six percent grade.

The closer we got to Wolf Creek Pass, the more I found myself standing—up on my legs. The good thing was, they seemed to be getting stronger each day. It was a strange sensation to feel this increase in power. My legs always have been quick but never large or strong. In elementary school I was often the last person left in the dodgeball circle. I was speedy! Because of my agility, I was given the nickname "Shifty." Not a very flattering handle, perhaps, but in the preadolescent world of "Butch" and "Fats" and "Big Foot," "Shifty" didn't seem so bad. Later, in my college years, a group of friends on my birthday presented me with a trophy for "the world's skinniest legs." Some friends! To witness today that these thin appendages were propelling me across the country would have amazed them all!

The second hill, Hesperus, was touted as the more difficult, but in truth it seemed easier. We made it to the top of the hill by noon and looked forward to the eleven-mile, six percent downgrade from there into Durango. What a ride! We peaked at over forty-four miles per hour, even with the wind at our side. At those speeds the wheels are spinning at about 550 revolutions per minute and you have to watch for every bump and rock. A stray stone or surprise crease in the road can easily result in a wicked, nasty crash or, in biker's lingo, a "biff."

Speaking of crashes, the bikers at the Cannondale web site (www.cannondale.com) have come up with the following terms you can use the next time you fall off your bike: schmucked, snorked, yerked, doinked, munched, hunted moles, dug for worms, chewed mud, went nose surfing, communed with the centipede gods, tasted the trail, got a free tattoo, ate a sidewalk sandwich, did a close-up geological survey, hugged earth, rode the nose hoe, got a topsoil makeover, made a gravity check [just to make sure it still works], became one with the Earth, did a flying dismount, added to my scab collection, used my face brake, sniffed soil, boned [i.e., hit so hard your flesh was ripped to the bone], and made dirt angels.

Happily, we had no cause to use our face brakes.

We had made arrangements to have lunch with Len Goebel and his wife, Eileen, in Durango. They took us to Francisco's Mexican Restaurant and we enjoyed a pleasant meal and conversation. Halfway through the meal Eileen said, "Len and I have a blended family and things haven't always been easy. Few people understand the unique struggles involved in raising a family that just 'happened' one day. *Focus on the Family* has been a godsend to us." Her words reminded me again of the awesome responsibility Dr. James Dobson carries each day behind that radio microphone. Radio waves may be invisible, but their influence can be enormous.

By 2:00 P.M. we were pedaling once more, this time on pavement doused by rain, the first real precipitation we'd had. Our feet were the first to suffer from the slow, steady drizzle. In measured succession our shoes, then our socks, and finally our feet became soaked. Our toes almost went numb as the air became colder and the moisture continued to fall. Speeding trucks and cars sprayed us with muddy water from head to toe and our velocity dropped to less than ten miles per hour. Coupled with terrain more hilly than expected, the sixty-one miles from Durango to Pagosa Springs—our last stop before crossing the Rockies—took us over five hours.

Therefore, despite the misspelling, I was grateful to read a sign posted at the True Value Hardware store in Pagosa: "Welcome Mike Troute to Pagosa Springs." We needed to dry off and get cleaned up right away, because we had been invited to dinner at the Power House, a youth ministry overseen by Bay and Peggy Forrest. First Timothy 4:12 is the group's motto: "Don't let anyone look down on you because you are young, but set an example for the believers in speech, in life, in love, in faith and in purity."

Bay is a former professional basketball player with the Phoenix Suns who toiled during the Alvin Adams era in the 1970s. When Bay retired, he and Peggy decided they wanted to do something significant with their lives. They knew they'd like to work with youth and, after pondering several possibilities, they chose Pagosa Springs as the site for their new ministry. Pagosa is small enough (population 12,000) that no single church is big enough to generate a large, thriving youth group. Bay and Peggy operate a nondenominational ministry that appeals to the youth of several local churches, thus providing a solid group to which large numbers of teens are attracted.

The ministry means so much to local residents that the owner of an old warehouse downtown leased his building to the Forrests for ten years at a cost of one dollar, with an option for another ten years. Over a period of several weeks volunteers gutted and remodeled the facility, and now Focus Ministries boasts a large, comfortable center equipped with foosball table, pool table, Ping-Pong table, old couches and chairs, a stage, and enough room to satisfy the boisterous meetings of both junior and senior high youth. A tremendous amount of ministry goes on in that place, and expansion plans are constantly being revised.

What makes the ministry so effective? "We gather hundreds of teenagers into one place and give them a positive identity," Bay explained. It was thrilling to hear so many stories of what is happening in the Pagosa Springs high school through the ministry.

"These teenagers have become very effective in sharing Christ with their fellow classmates," one supporter told us. "They're growing both personally and spiritually and are bringing their unsaved friends to the Lord."

Bay and Peggy also understand that small town ministry will probably look different from what might be found in the nation's megacities, so they tailor what they do to fit the community they serve. "But we also hope that what we're doing might serve as a model for other communities about our size," Bay said. "If it works so well here, there's no reason it shouldn't work in similar places."

All of this generates tremendous support from the community. Pastors from three churches joined us for dinner, and all three praised what God was doing through the Power House. Obviously, it's a tremendous asset to churches throughout the area.

Yet that made me wonder: how often do churches cooperate in supporting a youth ministry with no denominational bias? Bay and Peggy wonder, too, and hope that somehow they can share the lessons they've learned in Pagosa Springs with visionaries from other small towns who would like to create similar ministries in their own communities.[2]

Did you know that more than eighty percent of those who come to Christ do so before the age of eighteen? That's a telling statistic if ever there was one. Healthy, thriving youth ministries provide a broad avenue for searching teens to find new life in God through his Son, Jesus Christ. The more cutting edge ministries there are in this country, the better off our nation will be. Bay and Peggy Forrest represent the thousands of dedicated youth workers who labor in various vineyards of the Lord, and I applaud their energetic efforts. The heart of this American beats faster when he sees the lives of kids touched so deeply by the gospel.

Face to Face with the Wolf

In the soft morning light the next day we discovered that Pagosa Springs is a delightful little town full of natural hot springs (and occasionally the accompanying sulfuric odor), quaint old homes with well-kept lawns, and beautifully groomed and maintained parks which seem to be connected, at least along the riverfront, with paved bike paths.

Yet as appealing as the town is, we didn't get up on May 20 to sightsee. That morning we arose to stare down the Wolf— Wolf Creek Pass, elevation 10,857 feet, the next major obstacle standing in our way to the Atlantic Ocean.

Fortunately, we would have company. Four members of Team Ironclad, a Christian cycling club from Pagosa Springs, along with their team leader and another serious racer, showed up at the motel early that morning to support our efforts. Eric Suttle, the team's leader, did some light maintenance on the bikes, cleaned the chains, and reoiled them. Four members of his team—Jeremy and Jason Humphreys, Darrin DeBoer, and Josh Ortega—would ride up Wolf Creek Pass with us on their mountain bikes. The youngest was fifteen, the twins eighteen. Just what I needed: more young, fresh legs to try to keep up with. Steve Meilicke, a recent graduate of Biola University and an accomplished racer, came to encourage us that morning but could not accompany us up Wolf Creek.

Team Ironclad was happy to join us up to the summit. I guess when you're young, torture is fun. But they were also training for a big international competition scheduled within the next few days. Competitors would race about forty miles from Durango to Silverton, competing within age groups and rankings.

We prayed as a group before we left the parking lot, then set off to conquer the mountain. At least it wouldn't be hot; temperatures hovered in the fifties and skies were largely overcast, threatening showers again.

As we started out I couldn't help but think briefly of my uncle's assault on this pass just two years before. It was May 7, 1995, and despite the calendar Tom's climb almost had to be aborted because of heavy snow. At first he tried to follow the tire tracks of passing cars—that was the only place he could find bare pavement—but soon even that strategy failed. He turned around and started back down the mountain, resigned to the idea that he'd have to try again the next day, when he spotted a snowplow making its way up the steep slope. He fell in behind it and ground his way slowly up the last three or four miles of the climb. Near the summit he was greeted by a ten-foot bank of snow on both sides of the highway which completely covered the wooden signs identifying the location of the Continental Divide. A group of people snapping pictures of the snow stopped long enough to clap and offer him their congratulations when he finally crested the summit.

Climbing Wolf Creek Pass was definitely the toughest ride we had yet made, but I was hoping we wouldn't have to tackle snow as well. We had to climb nearly 3,000 feet in about eight miles at a seven percent incline and elevations in excess of 10,000 feet. Most of the time I pushed up at about five or six miles per hour, willing myself to continue. I kept remembering the words of Tom Ritchey as I climbed. "Just keep pushing," I heard him say. "When your body says, 'Stop!' you need to keep going. And when your mind says, 'Stop!' you need to keep going, because your body can continue." So that's what I did. Fortunately, everybody else took a breather once in a while, and I didn't want to appear antisocial by refusing to join in.

Brian reached the summit about 1:00 P.M., sweating like crazy. Just as he crested the peak, an elderly couple in an RV with Illinois plates motored up to the summit sign, popped out, snapped each other's pictures, gave a whoop of victory, then hustled back into their warm vehicle and drove off in triumph. I made it to the top several minutes later, just missing the pleasant weather that until then had kissed the mountain. It didn't seem fair. Minutes before I arrived, it was bright and sunny with a few fluffy clouds; by the time I made it to the top, the temperature had dropped twenty degrees and it began alternately to rain, snow, and sleet, the whole sloppy mess driven along by a stiff, frigid wind.

Welcome to Wolf Creek Pass

Of course, the four guys from Team Ironclad reached the summit long before we did, but I had made it! It was a long, hard climb, but there I was, posing with five other cyclists beside the sign that proclaimed we had conquered every last one of the 10,857 feet to the summit of Wolf Creek Pass. For just a moment every other success in my life paled by comparison. This was a personal victory. I hadn't sprinted to the top, edging out a worthy opponent for a photo finish; there weren't grandstands filled with spectators gong berserk as I raised my arms in triumph. Actually, had I let go of the handlebars at an point, I would have toppled over in an ignominious heap. No, this was an accomplishment that only I was celebrating . . . a moment I will reflect upon in years ahead. When failures occur I can say, "But remember when I glided over the peak at Wolf Creek?" Someone has said, "If you try and fail, destroy any evidence that you tried." I wanted pictures of this. I tried and made it, with the key being *I tried.*

What a challenge! I was very pleased with my cycling progress. My pre-ride exercise regimen certainly paid off; I could see definite improvement in the strength of my legs and my ability to oxygenate my blood. Although I was dog tired, that wasn't the thought uppermost in my mind. Another word had taken center stage, crowding out all others: *Encouraged.*

I had stared down the Wolf, and now he was at my feet. My very, very cold feet. Only one desire remained.

Where's lunch?

We loaded the bikes in the van and descended the mountain to eat in South Fork. By the time we drove back to the summit and Brian and I remounted our bikes, the storm had passed, leaving only dark clouds and cold temperatures in its wake. Soon we were hurtling down the mountain, but immediately noticed that our bikes shook so violently we thought they were about to disintegrate—until we realized that they shook only because *we* were shivering . . . and hard! The problem was not the bikes, but *us!*

Slowing down wouldn't help; cold is cold. Later I recalled an afternoon many years earlier in Burbank, California, when I was also on a bike, only this time delivering newspapers as a ten-year-old. A cold drizzle fell steadily, making the streets slick. I was miserable. To keep my papers dry I had to put them in plastic bags, which delayed my departure. So now my customers would get antsy. People were always anxious to get their afternoon edition of the *Burbank Daily Review*. How else would they know what was on sale at Hugh's Market? I raced through my route, wishing my mom could drive and keep me warm and dry in the car. My wool Pendleton shirt and cotton jacket clung to my upper body like a soggy Kleenex. As I tossed the last paper as close to a porch as possible, I headed my balloon-tired Schwinn toward home, my wet and freezing body shivering all the way. The bike shook then, too, and my hands felt numb. I was home in less than ten minutes, however, and warmed up in thirty. Obviously, that wasn't going to be the case for Brian and me as we cautiously raced down the east side of Wolf Creek Pass.

Just beyond Del Norte we ran into heavy rain and hail. Earlier we had sent the van ahead into Alamosa to find a motel with a hot tub, so neither Ted nor Steve knew we were freezing, wet, and miserable. Water collected along the side of the road and we often pushed through puddles six to eight inches deep. By the time we dragged ourselves into town, we were more than anxious to jump into a warm shower.

Alamosa was something of a nonentity. One part of town literally could be termed "the other side of the tracks." On one side are the new developments, the strip malls, the nice roads and

Brian and I officially begin our journey by dipping the rear tires of our bikes into the Pacific Ocean. *(top)*

As we leave the pier, we're off on our cross-country adventure! *(left)*

Nothing can distract us now—not even the lively scene on the Santa Monica pier. *(below)*

Our first "historical" rest stop—The San Fernando Mission. *(right)*

You'd sweat, too, if you were pedaling under a blazing California sun! *(below)*

Our second day of riding brought another day of intense heat and bright sunshine. *(bottom)*

Oh, yeah! Oh, yeah! This is good. Oh, yeah! I ducked out of the sun for a few precious minutes. *(left)*

Up, up, and away to Oatman, Arizona. *(bottom left)*

There's at least one burro in Oatman who has developed a taste for Peak Bars. *(below)*

Our first major milestone—Brian and I conquer the summit at Sitgreaves Pass, Arizona. *(bottom right)*

Welcome To
OATMAN ARIZONA

You're just a few minutes away from a step back in time. Feed the wild burros, visit the Shops, and have a great day.

SITGREAVES PASS
ELEV. 3550

We begin Day 7 of our adventure with the Grand Canyon looming in the background. *(right)*

Brian and I enjoyed a great lunch with Karen Landis, a wonderful hostess and true cowgirl from Seligman, Arizona. *(below)*

As dusk fast approaches we're still several miles outside our stop for the night in Tuba City, Arizona. *(bottom)*

Four Corners is the only place in the United States where four states meet at a single point. *(left)*

The Oliver Wang family of Taipei, Taiwan, wanted to know why we were biking across the United States. *(below)*

Brian and I pose for the camera just outside our motel rooms at the Anasazi Inn in Tsegi Canyon. *(bottom)*

Colorado brings us our first significant rain of the trip. *(right)*

We were grateful that our support van seldom ventured too far away from us. *(below)*

The Power House—a successful outreach ministry led by Bay and Peggy Forrest in Pagosa Springs, Colorado—draws students and supporters from throughout the community. *(bottom)*

Energetic members of Team Ironclad, a mountain biking team from Pagosa Springs, accompanied Brian and me to the summit of Wolf Creek Pass. *(top)*

Brian and I prepare for our assault on the highest peak we must scale on our entire journey. *(left)*

Victory at Wolf Creek Pass—all 10,857 feet of it! *(bottom)*

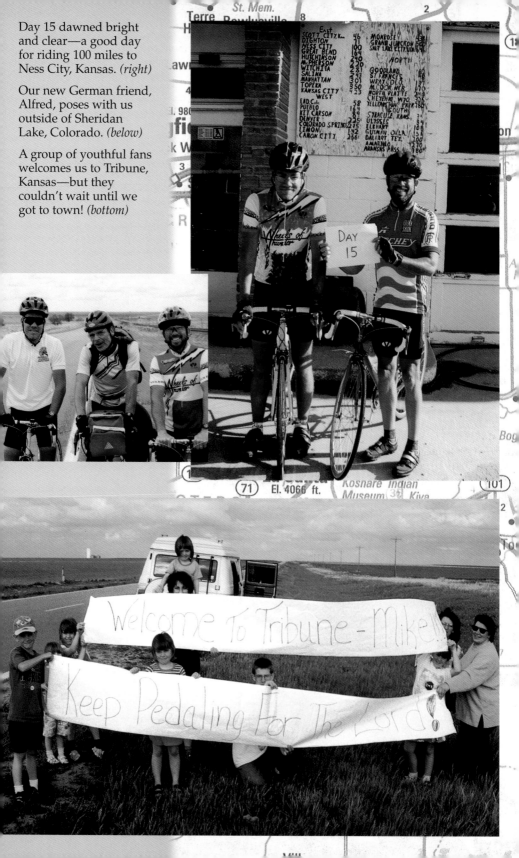

Day 15 dawned bright and clear—a good day for riding 100 miles to Ness City, Kansas. *(right)*

Our new German friend, Alfred, poses with us outside of Sheridan Lake, Colorado. *(below)*

A group of youthful fans welcomes us to Tribune, Kansas—but they couldn't wait until we got to town! *(bottom)*

Doris and Dale Nitzel provided us with a fabulous Sunday afternoon meal at their bed and breakfast in Great Bend, Kansas. *(left)*

All across the country we met new friends eager to lend their assistance, such as the good folks at the First Methodist Church of Leoti, Kansas. *(below)*

"Christ Pilot Me" said the white Kansas stones, and our Lord did just that on Day 16 of our adventure—a day that ended with multiple tornadoes. *(bottom)*

WELCOME TO LEOTI

MIKE TROUT - FOCUS ON THE FAMILY
FRI 8 00 POTLUCK AT METH CHURCH

* GRAND OPENING KANSAS CELLULAR *
FRI. M - D COMMUNICATIONS

KSKZ FM 99.9

Bob Dorris from Erie, Kansas, spends many of his retirement days building dinosaurs out of old car and truck parts. *(top)*

Kansas is home to the first Christian martyr in North America and boasts a rich spiritual history that too many of us overlook. *(center)*

A crowd at the Walmart parking lot in Newton, Kansas, was curious to hear about our trip, now halfway completed. *(bottom)*

Memorial Day at the Whitewater Cemetery filled me with gratitude for all those who lost their lives in the fight to protect our freedom. *(bottom inset)*

In Poplar Bluff, Missouri, we were treated to an outdoor reception sponsored by radio station KOKS, 89.5 FM. After our reception I was interviewed by KOKS. *(top)*

"Why did I take this trip? Well, it beats me!" Actually, here I am answering a few questions from a crowd of about 75 gathered at Northtown Mall in Springfield, Missouri. *(center)*

A reception outside of Knoxville, Tennessee, at Cedar Springs Christian store—the largest independently owned Christian bookstore in the country—gave us the opportunity to meet a number of folks interested in our bike trip across the nation. *(bottom)*

Day 28 of our trip found us leaving Tennessee—only a few more days of riding left! *(right)*

Coming upon this famous trail was a real thrill because it meant we were getting closer to our final destination. *(below)*

The Appalachian Mountains make up in distance and accompanying wind what they lack in sheer height. *(bottom)*

Brian, Ted, and I say goodbye to radio station WMIT in Asheville, North Carolina, as the mist closes in on the Blue Ridge Mountains. *(left)*

A wet, dreary day prompted us to take a needed day of rest at the Ridgecrest Conference Center outside of Asheville, North Carolina. A welcome rest indeed! *(bottom)*

Billboards and signs posted across America spell out the fervent religious faith of a great number of this nation's citizens. *(right, below)*

Wherever we went, people turned out to encourage us. Some, like this family, showed up ready to ride. *(bottom)*

Problems? Holy Bible

Follow The Instructions!

WHERE WILL YOU SPEND ETERNITY SMOKING OR NON SMOKING

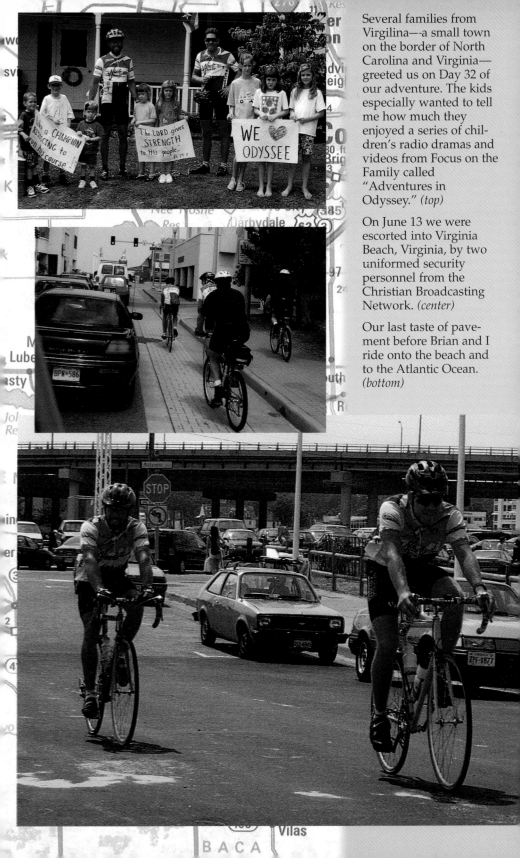

Several families from Virgilina—a small town on the border of North Carolina and Virginia—greeted us on Day 32 of our adventure. The kids especially wanted to tell me how much they enjoyed a series of children's radio dramas and videos from Focus on the Family called "Adventures in Odyssey." *(top)*

On June 13 we were escorted into Virginia Beach, Virginia, by two uniformed security personnel from the Christian Broadcasting Network. *(center)*

Our last taste of pavement before Brian and I ride onto the beach and to the Atlantic Ocean. *(bottom)*

June 13, 3:10 p.m. The front tire's in the ocean! And the adventure has been completed! What can I say, but "Praise the Lord!" *(right)*

Note to anyone who thought I couldn't do it: That's Brian and me there with our bikes in the air, celebrating our coast-to-coast triumph. WE HAD DONE IT! *(bottom)*

sidewalks and schools. On the other side are decay and increasing squalor. It didn't occur to me at the time, but in some ways the town reflected the way Brian and I were beginning to feel.

We were getting progressively fatigued with less and less sleep each night, and we had yet to take a day off. I knew I wasn't gaining weight, but my body felt heavier. It took more and more effort to lift myself out of bed each morning. It felt as though some miniature imp had tied me down at night with thin threads. I could break through, but each day required greater effort. And I was reminded of an old Gary Larsen cartoon. Two spiders have spent the night weaving a web at the bottom of a playground slide. Way back in the distance we see some plump kids running toward the slide. And one of the spiders says to the other, "Man, if this works, we'll eat like kings for a week." I felt as if I'd been caught in the web at the end of the slide. The only thing that regularly pushed me up and out of bed was the knowledge that Steve and Ted probably already had showered and packed and were ready to go.

I've learned my lesson. If I ever take another trip like this, I will make one major change in the way I lay it out: I'll be more careful about plugging Exodus 20:8–11 into my equations. The command to rest one day out of every seven not only makes good sense, it spares us all kinds of grief. Not just on bike trips, but in everyday life as well.

The Mountains Take Their Toll

May 21 would be a big day for us, not only because we would tackle the second major pass through the Rockies (La Veta, 9,413 feet) but also because Channel 5, the NBC affiliate from Colorado Springs, was to send a camera crew to film us on the road. This would be the second of three reports they would file on our cross-country trek. Groggy and a little cranky from too little sleep, we got on the road and began pedaling east under cool, cloudy skies. Every morning before heading off on the bikes we took a picture of Brian and me, and the one taken on this morning told the whole story: Where smiles usually lit up our faces, on this day nothing appeared but grim resignation. Soon a light rain was falling.

About noon, reporter Michael Chisholm of Channel 5 Eyewitness News stopped us just outside of Blanca for a roadside interview. We ate lunch at Del's Diner, near Fort Garland at the base of La Veta Pass. The TV crew followed us inside and continued its interview there. These TV guys are slave drivers. They came in and more or less took over. Everyone in the diner was looking around quizzically; it looked as if we were shooting a movie. After the film crew got what it needed, its members also grabbed a bite to eat and then took off to find another place to shoot some footage closer to the pass.

Freezing rain followed us all the way from Del's Diner to the summit of La Veta Pass. The news crew filmed us riding in the rain—yet another miserable ride. This was our third straight day of inclement weather.

Yet God often has a way of bringing some sunshine into even the most cloudy of days. Just before we reached the summit of La Veta, an older couple pulled up alongside the van as it waited for us beside the road.

"Is this the Mike Trout van?" the driver asked.

"Yes, sir," Ted replied.

"Well, hello," the man said. "I'm Bill Cullor, and this is my wife, Marge. Where is Mike? We heard of his trip on *Focus on the Family*, and we were hoping to find him up here and maybe hook up with him. I guess we'll go look for them. We'll be back!"

And with that they were off.

Brian and I caught up to the van a short time later and stopped to put on another layer of clothes and some dry socks. While we were changing, Bill and Marge came up behind us. Bill got out and introduced himself.

"Oh, Mike, it's such a privilege to meet you," he said with an enthusiastic handshake. "Marge and I are longtime *Focus on the Family* listeners. When we heard about your trip, we called *Focus* to find out where you were supposed to be by this afternoon." We learned later the Cullors have listened to *Focus on the Family* since the program first went on the air in 1977. They've been married for fifty-five years.

The broad smile covering Bill's face seemed undimmed by the rain, which was still falling. "You see," Marge pitched in, "it's going to be Bill's birthday tomorrow and each year we try to come up with something special to celebrate. When we heard about your trip, Bill said, 'Why don't we go down and meet up with those crazy guys on the bikes and spend my birthday with them?'"

So that's what they did. "Would you mind if we joined you at your motel tonight and chatted awhile?" Bill asked.

"Oh, please do," I said. "We're staying at the Days Inn in Walsenburg." That was all the encouragement they needed. They happily took off to book their own room along with our family members who would join us in Walsenburg. Shortly afterward we sighted Brian's parents, Marty and Dorian Slivka, along the side of the road, and they briefed us on the motel and who would be staying where. We kept pedaling and soon passed a large nativity set nestled inside a sandstone cave; in front stood three six-foot crosses. What a great welcome to this evening's destination.

It had been almost two weeks since we left home to begin our adventure, and it was great to have our loved ones with us even for a few hours. For me, it brought the real world back. We were out on the road, on bikes, and had become part of the horizon; we weren't traveling toward it, we were a part of it. But when we reached Walsenburg and saw Brian's family off to the side of the road, it was like a reality check.

Author George Gilder marshals some impressive evidence to claim that women are the ones who keep men civilized; if it weren't for women, he says, most of us men would live very irresponsibly. Men who are away from their families for a long time often lose that mooring and baser thoughts begin to take over. I've always thought that if men weren't commanded in the Bible to take leadership responsibilities, we would abdicate that role to women in a heartbeat. Seeing my wife and family out there brought me back to civility.

The night was made even more special by the presence at dinner of Marge and Bill Cullor. We celebrated Bill's seventy-seventh birthday, sang "Happy Birthday" to him, and took several pictures. Steve noticed the "B–24 Liberator" cap Bill was wearing and mentioned that his own father had flown in B–24s during World War II. "Is that right?" Bill said. After further discussion they discovered that Bill was based out of the same island where Steve's dad, Bob, helped refuel Allied bombers. It's quite possible that Bob Halliday refueled the B–24 that Bill Cullor flew in!

It was a great night of family, laughter, storytelling, and good friends. And, of course, it didn't hurt that both Wolf Creek and La Veta were behind us.

Radio Days

The next morning we got one of our earliest starts of the trip. Brian and the morning crew from Magic FM, the Colorado Springs radio station that was helping him raise money for scholarships to Kids Across America, left Walsenburg about 7:30 A.M. I took off about five minutes later with Marilyn Wells, who was joining us on the road for a couple of days. Marilyn is Marlen's wife and an extremely accomplished cyclist in her own right. A former member of the Canadian cycling team (and a two-time Canadian national champion), she also raced twice in the now-discontinued women's division of the Tour de France, finishing eighth overall in the 1984 tour.

My daughter Rebekah forms half of Magic's morning crew; she and the other half, Chris Knight, planned to ride twenty miles or so with us, doing part of their morning show live from the road. That meant we'd barely crawl along, but the speed deficit would be worth it. That morning they raised more than $500 for camp scholarships earmarked for inner-city kids. One little girl stopped by to give us four quarters and a handful of pennies, while a trucker listening to the radio pulled over in his big semi and handed Brian a twenty-dollar bill. As he leaned out the window he shouted over the idle of his growling diesel engine, "I love you guys!"—meaning Chris Knight and Rebekah. "I listen to you all the way to the Kansas border. I wish there was a station like yours where I live." I felt like I'd just witnessed a piece of Americana. A hardworking trucker stopping in the middle of "cow country," handing perfect strangers money because he liked a radio station and wanted to help some inner-city kids. That spoke of freedom and compassion at the same time. And at the heart of that exchange was radio.

Radio has been at the center of an information- and entertainment-hungry America since the election victory of

President Warren G. Harding was broadcast in 1920 over KDKA, Pittsburgh. If you remember the golden days of radio, from 1930 to 1950, you no doubt recall the radio in your living room as the focal point of family activity. The world entered millions of homes through that portal, made of wire, wood, and glass. Today billions of radios serve the needs of listeners around the world. Imagine a globe without radio. Every aspect of our lives would be impacted. Some might enjoy the slower, quieter lifestyle for a while, but our passion for sports, music, news, traffic, weather, and time would eventually drive us back to that "radio music box."

I've done my share of travel around this globe, and I've been amazed at how unique American radio is. Nowhere else do you find the variety and sheer volume (pun intended) that we enjoy across the dial. Some may call it excess; I call it part of our lifeblood as a nation.

Good weather blessed us all day even though it had looked a little ugly in the morning, but that didn't last. The ride itself was fairly easy. We saw a lot of cattle, both dairy and beef, and were serenaded by sweet birdsong. (We noticed that while cows don't generally look as we pass, horses do—for whatever that's worth.) As we moved east, the mesas of western Colorado grew ever smaller, replaced by flat plains and grasslands and wheat fields. Farmland stretched out before us, barren of the junipers and sagebrush so common just a few days before. Soon the terrain looked more typically Kansan than Coloradan. We heard the song of meadowlarks and other songbirds happy to roam the countryside, accompanied by the chirps and clicks of various crickets and grasshoppers and cicadas. We were in the country! And the Mojave Desert was a distant memory.

The weather was so pleasant and the terrain so even that Brian's dad, Marty, got out the mountain bike we carried in the van as a spare and joined us for a ride. For more than twenty years Marty served as a communications officer with the Air Force. He has since retired and works in the private sector. He's a level A racquetball player, which means he's *good*. He's always stayed fit and is an example of the military preparedness you hear about. So even though he hadn't trained for a long bike ride, his general fitness regimen enabled him to go farther than most. Our radio escort departed before noon, but Marty kept going. He gave up his ride after fifty-two miles, just five miles short of La Junta. Toward the end he said he started cramping and his back side was killing him. Well, that's not exactly how he described it, but if you've ever spent much time on a bike, you know what I mean.

In La Junta we ate lunch at the Hogs Breath Saloon, a favorite local restaurant (the eatery's slogan: "Hog's Breath is better than no breath"). Our family joined us there, then returned to Colorado Springs.

Once again, we were on our own.

Descent Toward the Heartland

In most parts of the nation, towns greet visitors with the name of the town and its population. In this part of Colorado, you don't get population; you get elevation. It was no surprise, but I was interested to note the steeply declining elevations as we pulled away from the Rockies: La Junta, 4,066 feet; Las Animas, 3,901; Lamar, 3,622. Even that data told me we were moving in the right direction.

After 125 miles we stopped next to an enormous feedlot where thousands of cattle spent their last days doing nothing more than standing and eating and getting fattened for slaughter. It was dark and starting to rain, so we called it quits, got in the van, and drove the remaining eight miles into Lamar. We arrived just behind a severe thunderstorm that had dumped torrents of rain on the area.

By the end of our second week of riding, the West finally was beginning to recede and the nation's heartland was coming into view. As we mounted our two-wheeled steeds on May 23, the temperature hovered comfortably in the sixties and the sun shone in a blue sky dotted with fluffy, white clouds. The forecast called for heavy rains farther east, and already we could see far more clouds in that direction—our destination— than to the west. Not a good sign! The winds were doing their thing, and we'd just have to get used to it.

But soon the winds shifted and grew too strong to buck. It became clear that if we were to make our hundred miles, we'd have to get some help. And the best help in this case—barring the ability to coax the wind into another direction—was motor pacing (or drafting) behind the van. We lined up three across behind the van—Brian, Marilyn, and me—just inches away from the bumper. As Ted crept up to twenty-five miles per hour, we noticed an immediate improvement. It's amazing how much easier pedaling becomes when you're not battling a stiff wind.

Using the van as a windbreak does nothing for other travel hazards, however. Two territorial canines briefly chased us on our jaunt up to Highway 96, but they gave up their pursuit when their master called them back to his tractor. A while later a rattlesnake sunning itself in the road struck at Brian, but the fangs caught nothing but air. And thus the miles rolled on— brown grassland to our left, brown corn stumps to our right, now giving way to foot-high green wheat fields. A red eight-wheel tractor lay unused to our left; on our right, fallow fields.

Eventually our journey was interrupted by another cyclist heading toward us—a fellow traveler, it turned out, also a long way from home. A very long way!

Alfred hailed from a town about a hundred kilometers south of Frankfurt, Germany, and was biking across the United States using the bicentennial route, starting in Newport, Virginia. His trek would take him north to Wyoming and Montana, finally ending in Seattle. He was anxious to see the mountains. Never before had he seen the kind of terrain that surrounded him now, the dry farmland of eastern Colorado and western Kansas. The land is so arid here that farmers must let their fields lie fallow every other year to gain enough moisture to be useful.

Alfred had taken two months off of work (one month of vacation, the other unpaid leave) and had left his wife and grown children back home to pursue his American adventure. As someone who is dedicated to serving the needs of the family, I was glad to hear that Alfred was calling his wife every couple of days to let her know that "I am still living, still on the earth." The year before, after he had decided to take this trip, he taught himself English. He was grateful that English is so much easier to learn than German.

Eventually Alfred asked about our names. "Mike," I said. "Oh, very American name," he replied in his thick German accent. When we introduced Marilyn he exclaimed, "Oh, Marilyn Monroe!" I think I nearly convinced him that our Marilyn was the late Miss Monroe's sister—her very, very much *younger* sister. Hey, they're both blonds, aren't they?

With introductions complete, we offered Alfred three Peak Bars, after which he promptly declared, with much conviction, that Americans were "the nicest people in the world." The night before, he told us, he'd been in Tribune, Kansas, and ran headlong into some rugged weather about six miles outside of town. A passing motorist gave him a ride into the city and took him to a motel. After Alfred cleaned up a bit and stowed his gear, he headed to the office to pay for his room—whereupon the attendant informed him that the person who had given him a lift already had paid for it. A modern-day tale of the Good Samaritan, played out on the Kansas plains!

As we prepared to resume our day's travel, our new German friend told us he thought something else was wonderful, too—the Mexican plate featured on the lunch menu at the Wheatland Cafe in Sheridan Lake, just fifteen miles from the Kansas border. "I never had so much food," he confessed. Not only was it delicious, but it gave him something to consume along with the twelve or more aspirin a day he took to relieve his acute riding discomfort. "Is very painful, where I sit down," he explained. We understood. Nevertheless, as we said our good-byes our friend wore a huge smile on his face and proclaimed he was having the time of his life. And we understood that, too.

The "lake" in Sheridan Lake promises more than it delivers, at least at this time of year. It's really more of a mud hole than a sizable body of water. When we reached the town, at Alfred's recommendation we stopped for a late lunch at the Wheatland Cafe. By that time the Mexican plate lunch special was gone. While waiting for our meals we were approached by Doug Wedekind, his wife, and their two children. Doug is the production director at KJIL, a popular Christian radio station based in Meade, Kansas. Doug had contacted us prior to our trip, asking to ride along for a short distance. Marlen Wells also joined us at Sheridan Lake, bringing his and Marilyn's son, Marty, who is four.

After a hearty lunch, four of us—Marlen (replacing his wife, Marilyn), Doug, Brian, and I—mounted our bikes once more and headed toward Tribune, Kansas.

CHAPTER 5

Drafting Through Kansas

"Mike Trout—Welcome to Tribune, Kansas!"

You haven't lived until you've seen your name in lights. Well, maybe not lights, but a pretty neat "billboard" by the side of the road.

That was the message that greeted us by the side of the road, held aloft by the eager hands of a vanload of kids. We were still more than an hour from Tribune—remember, that's less than thirty miles by bicycle—but the kids' mothers told us the youngsters just couldn't wait anymore. "We weren't sure when you'd arrive, so we've been ready for a couple of hours!" one mom told me. With squeals of glee everyone had piled into a van, headed west, and pulled over when they saw three cyclists pedaling hard toward another night's rest.

This was our first encounter with "an adoring public," and I was humbled by their show of interest and affection. Everyone is busy, no matter where they live, but here on the Colorado-Kansas border we were a priority for these folks. You know, it doesn't take much to lift someone's spirits. In this case, a little Midwestern hospitality and a paper banner was enough for us!

We snapped a picture of this heartwarming welcome and moved on, finally reaching the Tribune city limit as the sun began to sink in the west. We had planned on biking all the way into Leoti, but the headwind that snarled and snapped in our faces all day forced us to end our ride about twenty miles short of our goal. By the time we stopped for the night we had just enough time to check into our motel, clean up, and find the First United Methodist Church of Leoti, where a potluck had been arranged for us.

Leoti is primarily a farming community, with wheat the main crop. There's also big business in sunflower seeds and sunflower oil, and some in milo. We quickly learned that farms in the Leoti area are getting larger for at least two reasons. First, it's getting more difficult to earn a living by farming; the only way to survive is by operating ever-larger farms. "Economy of scale" plays a huge role here. Second, as technological advances in farm machinery continue to change agricultural practices, single families can take care of more land. The farmers we talked to in Leoti all noted the trend, some with more than a little worry. They wonder if the day is soon coming when they'll have to sell their farms and transition into some other kind of work—not a welcome prospect for Kansans who have been working the soil for decades, even generations.

We drove into Leoti and found the church, where thirty or so folks warmly greeted us, eager to hear about our journey. A number of young people were present and I grew deeply impressed that when Kansas families do something together, they do it *together*. One wheat farmer introduced us to his oldest son, who said, "I play football in high school and work out hard, but I can't imagine riding one of those skinny little bikes all the way across the country." As far as I could tell, none of the teenagers seemed at all perturbed that their parents expected them to show up at some potluck for a couple of weird guys bicycling in from who knows where. All evening long they were talkative and respectful.

I don't know how many of these kids' fathers held positions of authority in their churches, but I'm convinced they'd pass with flying colors one of the New Testament's bedrock qualifications for church leadership: "[An overseer] must manage his own family well and see that his children obey him with proper respect. (If anyone does not know how to manage his own family, how can he take care of God's church?)" (1 Tim. 3:4–5). At Focus on the Family we hear all the time about "wild" and "disobedient" teens, about young people who not only disobey their parents but who disrespect them in the most sad and shocking ways. You hear deep anger when they speak of their folks. One son wrote, "All my Dad does is yell at me. Everything is a big deal. We never have a normal conversation. I hate it!" Anger is the worst disciplinary tool a parent can wield and almost always yields devastating results.

But I don't want to recount any horror stories here; right now I want to celebrate and congratulate the parents and children of Leoti, Kansas, who honored us at First United Methodist Church. Hollywood can sneer at the rural lifestyles and traditional values of churchgoing farm folk if it wants to, but I know from experience that there's nothing like spending a few delightful hours with a group of young people and their parents who love God and obviously enjoy each other. If this is cornball, bring me a second helping!

After a delicious dinner I was asked to describe our adventure. I answered a few questions, then our cycling party stood in a circle so our hosts could lay hands on us and pray for us that the remaining portion of our trip would unfold safely and that all would go well.

At its heart, this is a praying nation. In times of great stress and difficulty, even the most hardened individual turns toward an almighty God and pleads for answers. As we felt the hands of these good people rest upon our shoulders, I thought of the millions of prayers which have been uttered in settings similar to this. Prayers for husbands and wives, for pastors, for missionaries, for teenagers and newborns. Presidents and mayors, teachers, coaches, doctors and nurses . . . all offering fervent petitions that have moved the heart of God. I am convinced that our trip went without serious incident because of the thousands of prayers lifted up on our behalf. John Wesley, the English evangelist who founded Methodism, once said, "God does nothing but in answer to prayer."

Although it was late when we returned to the motel, Marlen Wells insisted on staying up till the wee hours of the morning to work on our bikes, cleaning and oiling and getting them prepared for another day's ride. I have to admit, they needed it! By Leoti they were in pretty ugly condition from all the rain and mud we'd been through, yet we never expected Marlen to make such a generous offer—he was joining us the next day on the road and needed his sleep as much as we did. Even so, he spurned his bed for a few precious hours and instead got intimately acquainted with the dirt and grease and grime of a couple of filthy bicycles.

Wipeout!

They say misery loves company, but so do bicyclists. On Saturday, May 24, we had a lot of company. Seven bikers lined up outside the Tribune city limits that morning to challenge the Kansas winds for the right to move about a hundred miles east.

Among the riders were Randy Jost, an experienced cyclist who administers a local nursing home, and Don Hughes, the general manager of radio station KJIL. Two riders dropped out of the group after a few miles, but Randy and Don spent a good part of the day with us. I'm not sure Don really *wanted* to hang out with us that long—in fact, the original plan called for him to ride only as far as Leoti—but for the welfare of his station he had little choice. When he broadcast his intention to ride along with us, people began calling in and asking if they could join him and us for a portion of the day; that's how we ended up with the large group of riders. The day of the ride, station colleagues followed Don in a car equipped with cell phones for on-the-scene reports.

Riding twenty miles from Tribune to Leoti may not seem like much to experienced cyclists, but observers had to be impressed with Don's accomplishment. He chugged along the whole way on an ancient Schwinn he bought twenty-five years ago. The bike did not carry its years well; it looked and sounded as if each torturous mile would be its last. About nine miles into the ride, Don started complaining about the hills in Kansas, which in his eyes seemed monstrous: "Boy, not another hill!" From our perspective there just aren't too many honest hills in Kansas, but to someone who has not ridden in years, any slight incline is going to seem like Pike's Peak.

As the ride progressed, Don got tired and began to wobble a bit. Suddenly his front tire bumped into Marlen's back tire. The impact made him wobble more erratically and in moments he went down, crashing into the pavement. He badly skinned up his knee and was visibly shaken; it took him a while to settle down. He had been struggling along at twelve or thirteen miles an hour when he hit the pavement, right in the middle of the road. The accident could have been far worse. Although he struck his head quite hard, he was spared serious injury because he was wearing a helmet borrowed at the beginning of the ride from Randy Jost.

There was a silver lining to this mishap, however. After Don's next live report, listeners began calling in pledges for each mile he completed. His encounter with the pavement had jogged loose donations for KJIL's noncommercial budget. Within the next few minutes, contributions for each mile exceeded three-hundred dollars and Don ended up pushing beyond Leoti for a total of thirty-five miles (and more than ten-thousand dollars). What a wonderful ending to a potentially disastrous morning!

Signs of the Times

You get to read a lot of signs as you travel the country by bicycle. Visitors to Leoti are greeted by a sign that says, "Welcome to Leoti, A Great Place on the Great Plains." Outside Modoc, Kansas, a sign attached to the HRC feeder pens proclaims proudly, "Here's the Beef." A handmade sign indicates the meeting place of the Hispanic church "Templo de Alabanza, Alfa y Omega." Scott City entices passersby with "A historical past, a bright future." A sign on a cardboard box leaning against a weathered mailbox outside that same town read, "God speed, Mike Trout," while Dighton greets visitors with a hearty, "Welcome to Dighton! Shop 'til the cows come home."

Signs not only offer information and urge people to spend their money in certain ways, they often communicate something about the beliefs of those who put them up. We passed a great little African Methodist Episcopal chapel in Sterling, Kansas, that featured a sign hung over the front door instructing its parishioners to "Enter to Worship"—a little sign with enormous implications, too often forgotten. Another sign gracing the message board on the First Christian Church in Nickerson, Kansas, reminded passersby that "Experts made the Titanic; Amateurs made the ark." The sign reminds us that we are still free to take our pick today: safe passage on a divinely designed boat with Noah and his animals, or first-class comfort straight to the bottom of a frigid sea.

What we're willing to put up on signs often reveals what we are as a society. Here in Colorado Springs just the other day I heard a radio interview with the editor of the *Independent* newspaper, a liberal publication issued on weekends. When asked to name her favorite bumper sticker, the editor replied that "probably the most popular bumper sticker among readers of the *Independent* is 'Focus on your own damn family.'" Her personal favorite was "Celebrate diversity."

In contrast to that, I didn't see many liberal sentiments expressed in the signs and bumper stickers and billboards we encountered along our way, especially after Kansas. At least in the narrow ribbon of the country we saw, America is much more conservative than we are often led to believe.

Back to Drafting

We left for Ness City under sunny skies, the thermometer registered eighty-five degrees, with low humidity—but once more we faced a stiff headwind. Anyone for drafting?

This time we didn't use the van, but fellow cyclists. Our group of seven had dwindled to four, and Marlen and Randy led the way while Brian and I rode immediately behind them. By midafternoon, however, even this was not enough (plus, our "drafters" were getting tired). Marilyn scooted her car in front of us and maintained a steady pace of sixteen to twenty miles per hour. Soon we passed the younger of two brothers who had left Scott City on their bikes while we were eating lunch; we caught up with the older brother about ten minutes later. By that time, he was grateful to experience the blessings of drafting behind Marilyn's car.

The boys and their parents had introduced themselves to us at a restaurant in Scott City, where we enjoyed a late lunch with Don Hughes and several others. We had to hurry through our meal because the whole town was shutting down at 2 P.M. for the local high school graduation. The two boys wanted to race us to Dighton, so we encouraged them to get a jump on us by starting right then; we didn't hit the road for about forty-five minutes. We passed the younger boy after half an hour of riding and caught up to his brother less than two miles outside of Dighton. The group finally sprinted to the city sign. The oldest boy won (Marlen gave him a good push on the back twenty yards from the finish line). We stopped to say good-bye to everyone and took pictures. The boys' parents said they would all remember the day. It was a fun afternoon distraction spent with more new friends.

At Dighton, Randy left us to return home with his wife. "God bless you guys!" Marlen called out as the Josts drove away.

Halfway to the Atlantic

Ness City marks the only town outside of California in which we didn't stay in a motel. Not only are there few motels in this part of Kansas but the ones which do exist were full of softball players participating in a big tournament. Donna Lewis, my capable assistant at Focus on the Family, had arranged for us to stay with the King family.

Russell and Kristol King had arranged dinner for us at First Baptist Church, where Russell pastors. A group of about ten welcomed us, served another wonderful potluck, and provided an evening of conversation.

Most of these folks didn't know who we were; it was just their role in the church to offer hospitality to friends and strangers alike. Before we sat down to eat, we took a quick tour of the church. Attendance has grown over the years and a new section with added Sunday school rooms and a fellowship hall had been built in the previous few years. A single mom was pushing a vacuum cleaner in the sanctuary, putting last-minute cleaning touches on the building before Sunday services. She told me how the church had ministered to her and her children as they tried to make ends meet. Several years ago Focus on the Family began a monthly magazine just for single parents, and when this woman learned I was with the ministry, she bubbled over in gratitude for the publication.

"You can't know, until you've been through it, how lonely and desperate you can feel when you're single," she said. "Please tell those who put that magazine together each month that it's been a huge help to one mom out in Kansas." She then left the vacuum, picked up a pail and rubber gloves, and headed for the restrooms.

As I looked around the quiet sanctuary with its well-worn pews, I reflected on the people who would occupy these seats little more than twelve hours from that moment. Even in this small Midwest town, almost every human condition would be present. *This* is the hope of our country—people coming together, bringing their joys and sorrows, leaning on one another, praising God and seeking his guidance. And pastors everywhere have their spiritual work cut out for them.

When we returned to the new dining hall and sat down to eat, I was again struck by the polite behavior of the children, including the pastor's daughter and two sons. Could it be there's something in Kansas water that the rest of the country needs to gulp down in large quantities—as quickly as possible?

No, I suppose not. It has a lot more to do with how our children are reared. The King family, for example, had come to Ness City from Illinois in pursuit of a pleasant small town in which Russell could pastor a solid church and where he and Kristol could rear their children. They found all of these things in Ness City and have no desire to move elsewhere. I was amazed at their contentment in doing God's work away from any limelight. While they had the same concerns as many parents, they exuded a quiet trust in God to see them through. Once again, I felt that the picture of America that we often see on the evening news is distorted. There are a lot more decent, God-honoring people in this country than we realize.

Too soon, our evening ended and we went to the King home for a good night's sleep. The Wells family left us Saturday night after the meal; Marlen had to get back to Denver to teach a Sunday school class. Now it was back to just Brian and me, alone against the headwinds of Kansas.

We were more than half a continent away from our goal. To make it the next 1,800 miles or so we'd have to—you guessed it—do some drafting.

While much of America gathered that Sunday to worship God in churches across the land, Brian and I were drafting behind the van to get to another church in Great Bend, where we were expecting a noon potluck. When we finally pulled up to the First Church of the Nazarene, however, church was out and almost everyone had left—and they hadn't left behind any vittles. What had happened?

Someone ran from the parking lot into the church to look for Doris Nitzel, our contact, to find out the answer to this mystery. A mix-up had led Doris to believe we wouldn't be stopping by, so the church had canceled the potluck. Rarely have I seen anyone so apologetic for something not at all her fault. But Doris had a solution: Would we follow her husband and her to their home for dinner? It wasn't far. "I can fix a good lunch as quickly as any restaurant can. Won't you please join us for dinner?"

Do people really do this anymore? I've heard of families who, years ago, would have the "pastor and his family" over on Sunday afternoon, but I'd never experienced it myself. So there was something very personal about this opportunity, and we accepted eagerly.

Doris and Dale Nitzel have been running a bed-and-breakfast for eight years. They got the idea after visiting their daughter and son-in-law in Edinburgh, Scotland, where they stayed in a wonderfully memorable old B&B. The main portion of their house is more than a hundred years old, and for twenty-two years they've called it home. Out back in the garage, Dale has a rebuilt '46 Ford that is now equipped with electric windows, air conditioning, a handmade wooden dashboard, seats from a Mercury Cougar, and a 305 engine from a '77 Chevy. Not exactly stock; he's saving that for the '41 that sits a few feet away, awaiting its day for a new lease on life.

Doris's dinner showed pure Kansas hospitality. She served us corn from her own garden, ham from a pig they slaughtered, fresh strawberries, and homemade bread. She apologized for the "store bought" potatoes on our plates, tubers she clearly disdained; their own, she explained, hadn't come in yet. We assured her that everything, including the suspect potatoes, was excellent, and that she could certainly compete with the best restaurant in town. By 2:30 P.M we were off again, our stomachs full . . . and our eyes brimming with visions of dark clouds massing ahead.

Into Tornado Alley

I was born in Richmond, Virginia, and for my first four years lived just north of that in Ashland. I still have very fond memories of summer evenings spent in warm and humid climates. I recall playing outside, or enjoying a late evening dinner, and watching lightning bugs by the truckload flash on and off everywhere around me, like a thousand miniature paparazzi trailing a big movie star of the bug kingdom. Oftentimes, lightning itself in the distance would put on quite a display.

I recalled all this as we peddled through Kansas, thunderheads crashing all around us. The unique feel in the air, the fresh smell of the fields—all of it brings back the good times I had growing up.

Thunderstorms aren't mainly about memories, however. They're about rain. And wind. And hail. And lightning. And sometimes they're about tornadoes ... that is, real danger.

We began biking on this Sunday just grinding it out, earnestly hoping to get in as early as possible. By early afternoon weather forecasters were issuing tornado watches over a large portion of Kansas, including the route we were taking. At 5:25 P.M. a tornado warning—not merely a watch—was issued for northwestern Barton County, the county we just happened to be riding through. Soon the reports started coming in: A funnel cloud had been sighted north of Galatia, some thirty or forty miles away; a tornado had touched down just outside of Hays in Ellis County and was moving east-northeast at ten to fifteen miles per hour; yet another tornado was sighted in Claflin, twenty-five miles to the northwest. With each report it sounded as if the tornadoes were closing in on us, although we saw nothing but threatening clouds. So we biked on.

Thankfully, the twisters stayed away from our path and we stopped just outside the Lyons city limits. No sooner had we stowed our bikes and climbed into the van than half-inch hail and heavy rain began pounding us. It hailed so hard that we couldn't hear the van's radio, regardless of how loud we turned it up.

While we sat in the van, waiting for the storm to let up, my mind went back to one of the first sights to greet our eyes as we began our ride that day. Off to our right on the crest of a rounded hill stood three large crosses, gleaming in the morning sun. Beneath them in white stone letters were written the words "CHRIST PILOT ME."

And I thought: *Christ did pilot us today. He piloted us past all the tornado activity that's assaulting this whole area. He piloted us around lightning and he piloted us around hail. He's piloted us to this very moment and to this very spot, and now that we're safely in the van, he's allowed the heavens to open and pour down torrents of rain and hail.* And I prayed silently: *Lord, thank you for being our Pilot! Thank you for being with us today, for getting us safely here to Lyons. I didn't realize how dangerous it really was out there— thank you for your hand of protection.*

The next day we discovered just how dangerous it had really been. No fewer than fifty-one tornadoes had been sighted in Kansas, Colorado, Oklahoma, and Texas. According to news reports, one of those tornadoes seriously damaged the roof of Carl and Jo Johnson's home and demolished a nearby shed. Golf-ball-sized hail fell in Newton, twenty-five miles away. Gary Theurer's home near Wellington was destroyed— walls torn out, sections of a room ripped away, windows shattered, a board from the garage 200 feet behind the house embedded in the kitchen wall.

The real test of a community is how it responds to such a disaster, and these towns and small cities in the heartland passed their exam with straight A's. According to one report:

By mid-morning, about thirty cars belonging to neighbors and friends lined the gravel road near Gary Theurer's house.

Area farm wives brought sandwiches, cookies, and drinks for the workers. Men were clearing scrap metal from the downed barn and sheds. Others loaded the family's few undamaged items onto a red trailer for storage at a neighbor's place.

"Whether you're part of the family or not, you just start being part of the family," said Rosie Watts, a neighbor who watched the tornado move past her house.[1]

Additional help was offered by the Mennonite Disaster Service, assistance that Gary Theurer welcomed. Despite the damage, he was grateful, saying it could have been much worse.

"We still have all the family," said Theurer's mother, Mary. "That's the main thing. The other things can be replaced."[2]

It's hard to be grateful when disaster strikes, and no one is delighted over the deep pain catastrophes cause, but we can lift our praises to God when serious injuries are avoided and people come together in common cause to help their neighbors. Part of the reason I took this trip was to discover the heartbeat of America, and I think it's in the middle of human heartache that we make the most compelling discoveries.

So what did I learn on a stormy Sunday near Lyons, Kansas? That Christ continues to pilot his people today. That God is gracious and providentially cares for his children. That there are still an awful lot of good neighbors out there, men and women who are willing to put aside their own concerns for a while in order to help out a friend in need. And that the cherished character qualities of generosity, hospitality, and kindness are far from extinct in this nation, especially in America's breadbasket.

One Person At a Time

The Lyons Inn is owned and managed by a Christian couple named Charlie and Gloria Vondra. Both are very familiar with *Focus on the Family* and listen to the broadcast regularly. Quietly, without being pushy or intrusive, they put forward the Christian message. A wonderful little sign greets guests as they enter their rooms. If they have come for a family gathering, the sign hopes the event goes well; if they are there for business, it wishes them success; if they are there for a funeral or some other time of grief, condolences are shared. I have never seen anything like it and was impressed with both its touching empathy and its clear Christian sentiments.

Near the office counter where guests check out hangs a simple wooden container filled with various tasteful tracts supplied by the Gospel Tract and Bible Society of Moundridge, Kansas, a division of the Church of God in Christ, Mennonite. One such tract says in big, bold letters: "WANTED: Young Men and Young Women. Apply Now!" The leaflet then asks,

> Boys and girls, do you know the Lord Jesus is looking for you and calling you to come in and make application? First

of all, He wants to save you, make new, truly good persons out of you. Even though He is calling you, you must also submit your application. No boy or girl can possibly be saved unless they go to the Lord about the matter. Thousands are unsaved because they do not attend to this Number One step. Hear the announcement of the Lord Jesus: "Whosoever will, let him come." He does not invite only a few special ones. His grace embraces all.

How many boys and girls, men and women have been turned to the Savior because of such simple tracts? I have no idea, but God does. And one day he'll reward the writers of such tracts and those who give them out, such as the Vondras, for their faithful service to him.

Of course, Christianity is more than giving out the Good News of the gospel; it's also about living out that Good News. And here the Vondras also passed muster. Throughout our trip we tried to wash our riding clothes at least every other day, for obvious reasons. Although the Vondras did not have self-service laundry facilities for their guests, they let us use the commercial washer and dryer reserved for handling the motel's linens.

Charlie Vondra is a generous and gregarious man, but he has reason not to be. He had been a farmer all his life, but lost everything during the '80s. Inflation was running rampant and Charlie was speculating in land which, on paper, was worth over a million dollars. When the Reagan administration halted inflation and calmed down the economy, Charlie lost everything. "I'm not upset about it now," he said. "I was at the time, but I realized a lot more folks were helped when the economy turned around than were hurt." He transferred the farm to his children so that he and his wife could reap the tax benefits, then bought the motel, one of two in Lyons. Today he serves the needs of his guests and hopes that occasionally one of them might be pointed to the Lord Jesus Christ.

The Flags Come Out

Memorial Day dawned muggy and gray, with a forecast uncomfortably reminiscent of the day before. We got an early start and soon passed Whitewater Cemetery, decorated with scores of American flags flapping proudly in the wind. I doubt

I've ever seen Memorial Day celebrated as energetically and ubiquitously as it is in Kansas. The patriotism here almost looks religious in its fervency, but I found it enormously refreshing and quite encouraging.

When General John Alexander Logan first marked the end of May as a time to decorate the graves of those who had died during our nation's wars, he was thinking specifically of the Civil War. Kansas played a strategic role in the tragic journey toward that awful conflict. This centermost state in our "lower forty-eight" entered the union as a free state on January 29, 1861. Yet the Territory had been set aside in 1854 under the Kansas-Nebraska Act and slavery was allowed at the discretion of the area's inhabitants. A conflict known as the Border War erupted almost immediately between pro-slavery settlers from Missouri and anti-slavery homesteaders moving in from the northeastern states. One of the bloodiest battles was led by abolitionist John Brown just north of our bike route. The bitterness of that and other intense conflicts deepened the rift between North and South and accelerated the slide toward civil war.

On this cloudy Monday, Memorial Day 1997, I couldn't help but think of another war. Dr. Dobson and others call it a "civil war" of values. Our nation is once again engaged in a great conflict, this time for our moral soul. And while it is easy to point outward to blame all sorts of special interest groups, the real way to win this war is to look inward. What am I doing to bring hope and healing to my neighborhood? What are you doing? Only you and I can turn the tide in this country ... one person at a time.

New Game in Town: Keeping Up with Mike

From Lyons we headed south to Sterling where we picked up another rider, John Cooper. John hails from Hutchinson and asked his wife to drop him off in Sterling, about eight miles out of Lyons. We took several back roads on our way to Hutchinson and enjoyed our ride with John, although we paid for a casual comment made at the beginning of our trek.

We told John we had been averaging twenty to twenty-one miles per hour on our way down from Lyons, so John set exactly that pace. The trouble was, from Sterling on we were heading east and lost a slight tailwind. At first we rode along side by side, with John firing questions our way: "What's been the toughest part of the ride?" "Has anyone else ridden with you?" "Has the weather cooperated?" "How were the Rockies? I bet they were tough!"

Just as I'd push out a few words in response, he'd launch another barrage of questions. The farther we went, the harder it became to keep up. Eventually I drifted back toward Brian, who had allowed about a quarter mile to open up between John and me and himself. After several miles, we came upon John's wife, waiting for us at a quiet intersection.

"How're you all doin'?"

"Fine," I gasped.

"Where are you going to stop for breakfast?" Apparently she wasn't going to join us.

"Somewhere on this side of town, I suppose," I replied. I didn't relish the thought of chasing John through town and traffic! As she pulled away we said good-bye and John once again shifted into high gear. The previous day's storm had cooled temperatures, and I found myself wishing I'd dressed warmer that morning. Brian and I picked up the pace, eager to warm up quickly, and stayed about ten feet behind John all the way into town. Later he told us he was intimidated that we had ridden halfway across the country, and he wanted to make sure he "kept up." Next time someone asks me our pace, I'll hedge a little.

After breakfast John led us out of Hutchinson and to Highway 50 toward Newton. Once more, the wind had shifted. Another tough ride.

In Newton a crowd of about thirty welcomed us to the Wal-Mart parking lot. A local radio station conducted a short interview and I spent an hour or so talking to the folks gathered among the cars and answering their questions. It seemed that everyone, from kids to senior citizens, had a question about our trip. One gentleman was extremely interested in our bikes; he had ridden in the Bike Across Kansas event several times, but at eighty-one years of age, he wasn't sure he'd do it again.

"The fastest I've ever ridden was twenty-one miles per hour, and that was downhill with the wind to my back," he said. "At my age, speed makes me nervous."

Yet despite his doubts, he appeared to be quite fit physically; I'll be delighted if I can reach the age of eighty-one and still *remember* the last time I climbed on my bike to pedal across an entire state (even if by then I live in Rhode Island).

We were treated to lunch by Steve Reber, a young man who had arranged our gathering at Wal-Mart. Steve is a talented salesman for the Coca-Cola company but says he would love to be a youth worker for some Christian ministry. He reminded me of Marlen Wells, who had a similar passion and eventually left a career with the police force in Toronto, Canada, to attend Denver Seminary.

Steve told us, "I just want to do something with lasting impact. I see the pressures on kids today, and I think I can help." I wanted to tell him he could accomplish that goal without changing jobs, but my timing would have been off.

And I knew from my own experience that you never win if you put your own will ahead of God's. In 1978 I was scratching out a respectable living in the Los Angeles area by running my own production and broadcast consultancy business with two partners. Life was on an even keel in Southern California ... perhaps too even! When two friends in Chicago asked me to come and help run one of their radio stations, without much hesitation Nancy and I jumped at the new adventure. In October of that year we made all the necessary arrangements, waved good-bye to friends and relatives, and headed our new Ford Bronco toward Lake Michigan. As the Blizzard of '79—the coldest winter in Chicago history—began, these tanned Californians settled into an active suburban life. For the next two years we learned how to rake leaves, shovel snow, use the tollways, and dress for the windchill ... in that order. There were fresh opportunities for ministry! Truly the Lord had led us there.

Then another call came, this time from the West Coast. A station I had worked with was changing formats and asked if I would consider joining the new team.

Only in retrospect can I begin to understand our next move, for like a moth flying blindly toward the light, we said yes to the offer and turned on our heels (for all the wrong reasons) and retraced our path to Los Angeles.

After nearly ten roller-coaster months, I arrived home early one afternoon and announced that I was unemployed, something I had never known since my first job pumping gas at age sixteen. For the next eight months I eeked out a living through sporadic freelance work. I knew I'd taken a wrong step, and now my confidence was shaken. I cried out, "Lord, I let go the best I know how. Please take control!"

The next day a friend called with a serious lead. Apparently a young radio ministry in Arcadia, just east of Los Angeles, needed a person with management and production skills. After only a few questions about the job, however, I concluded it wasn't what I wanted (I was still on the up side of the "Lord's will" learning curve).

Sixty days later the same friend called with the same offer. A person had been hired but didn't work out . . . and this time I followed up. That was the summer of 1981 and I became the thirtieth employee of Focus on the Family. That process taught me a painful lesson: If our desire for the "greener grass" on the other side of the fence leads us to disregard the welfare of our family or to harbor bitter feelings of resentment or to grow lax in the responsibilities we have been given right now, then we can be sure we're not following the path God has laid out for us. We need to remember that a big part of seeking and securing and enjoying even God-given "greener grass" is our diligent faithfulness to the duties we have right now, at this moment.

"Are You Mike Trout?"

Our accommodations that night in El Dorado were paid for by John and Marsha Ashton, a delightful couple from Wichita. John is an accomplished cyclist, a racer in fact, and had vainly looked for us all day long. As we pedaled into the motel parking lot, a car was idling in the driveway with the driver's window down.

"Are you Mike Trout?" asked the woman behind the wheel. "Yes," I replied, and her face broke into a broad smile.

"We're sure glad we finally found you," she said. "We were beginning to get worried. I'm Marsha Ashton and this is my husband, John," motioning to the tall, lean man in the passenger's seat.

They waited for us as we prepared for a potluck at the First Baptist Church of El Dorado, arranged by another rider, Wes Hiebert. What a fabulous time! Our evening at First Baptist had to be one of the highlights of our trip. We found the people to be both engaging and hospitable. There's no question they follow in the footsteps of a celebrated El Dorado resident from many years ago, Brigadier General Alfred Washington Ellet. General Ellet is memorialized on a granite marker outside the Kansas Oil Museum in El Dorado and is described as "one of El Dorado's earliest settlers and up to the time of his death [in 1895], the city's leading and most illustrious citizen. He was a man of strong moral convictions and character. He opposed slavery and had the keenest sense of justice and right. He was a lover of his home, and of family, and a true patriot of his country."

I have little doubt that our hosts at the First Baptist Church can be equally so described. And the food they served was nothing short of outstanding. In particular I have in mind a dessert prepared by Renee Taylor, a member of First Baptist. All four of us on the trip—Brian, Ted, Steve, and I—not only raved about her dish but backed up our words with four or five trips to her serving bowl.

Renee's dish was so irresistible I decided the recipe had to be in this book. Try it for yourself.

Renee Taylor's Delicious No-Name Dessert
3 oz. package of vanilla instant pudding
1-1/2 cups buttermilk
8 oz. Cool Whip
1 can mandarin oranges, drained
15 to 20 oz. can of pineapple tidbits, drained
11 oz. package of fudge-striped cookies

Combine the contents of pudding mix with buttermilk, then fold in Cool Whip. Add the oranges and pineapple. Break cookies into dime-sized pieces and fold into mixture. (Can also add marshmallows and bananas if desired.) Refrigerate.

(You'll notice I didn't say how many this dish will serve. That's because most normal people, like me, will want to eat all of it themselves. So I could have said that it serves one, but that probably would give you the wrong idea.)

Although it had grown late by the time we said our good-byes, we came away from our time at First Baptist refreshed, energized, and grateful for new friends. We laughed a lot at dinner. Oh, how we laughed! And we needed that laughter; we hadn't laughed nearly enough on our trip. Proverbs 17:22 tells us, "A cheerful heart is good medicine," and we downed a lot of the stuff that night. I had a conversation with a big truck driver who was especially funny. He owned a classic Zenith radio and was trying to pry out of me information about its value; he had read somewhere that I collected antique radios. Immediately I recognized it as a marvelous collector's piece and jokingly began to explain to him that it really had very little value. "Oh, there are millions of them out there," I said. "But if you want me to take it off your hands, I'd be open to discussing the matter."

Beyond the superb company, the folks in El Dorado also provided us with some equipment assistance. After hearing about the number of tires we had trashed, someone got on the phone and tracked down the owner of a local Schwinn shop. This man then made a special late-night trip to his store, picked up the road bike tires he had in stock, and brought them to our motel to let us look them over (we bought one). He also looked over our maps with us and recommended the roads we should take as well as those we should avoid. Now that's customer service!

Guys Just Gotta Have Fun

The next day we arrived in Fredonia to the resounding clang of the bell on the courthouse clock. Although Fredonia sounds like it should be the name of a small Baltic country somewhere near Lithuania, it's really located at the rim of the scenic

Flint Hills. It was settled in 1868 by a man from Fredonia, New York, who named his little outpost after his hometown.

The town now claims about 2,500 residents; oil is a primary business. At one time a brick plant and a glass plant did booming business, but they have long since closed down. A cement plant still chugs along. Other than that, however, not much seems to feed the local economy. One wistful resident told us that Fredonia is basically a little town that struggles to stay alive. Somehow it manages to keep on going.

Fredonia presented us with our own challenge to keep going. For several days Brian had been having trouble with his bike. The bottom bearings in his pedal assembly were squeaking, indicating they might need to be replaced. We called Tom Ritchey and he helped diagnose the problem, but it was clear we'd have to hunt up a bike shop soon and see about getting some permanent repairs. In the meantime, we whipped out some WD-40 (one of America's two great fix-alls; duct tape is the other), squirted it in there, and hoped that would quiet things down. Then it was off to dinner and next to bed, where we hoped to find some real quiet.

Thankfully, we did.

One side benefit of riding a bike across the United States is that you get to eat more—no, you *have* to eat more. Physiologists estimate that cyclists burn about 500–600 calories per hour while riding, depending on their level of exertion and their weight. On flat terrain, with no wind and riding in an upright position, a 140 pound man in one hour burns about 502 calories riding at 15 miles per hour, and 828 calories at nineteen mph. Keep us that pace for six hours and your body requires an additional 3,000–5,000 calories per day. And remember, that's *on top of* what the body normally requires—a moderately active 155 pound man burns about 2,700 calories per day.

I can testify that hard cycling depletes the body of its energy reserves. I've reached that point cyclists call "bonking." It comes on very fast and is evidenced by a voracious appetite. If you don't eat something immediately, you could collapse—not a healthy event on a bike. To replace what they lose, wise cyclists must increase their intake of complex carbohydrates (sixty to seventy percent of total calories), and to a lesser degree, fat (twenty-five percent).

That, at least, is what the scientists and nutritionists tell us. So what does all this data boil down to? Just one thing: EAT!

The next morning, we piled into a booth at the Western Steak House in Fredonia. The restaurant had been recommended to us the night before and it seemed to be nearly the only place in town where visitors could grab a bite. What we grabbed was more than a bite. I've never seen such huge flapjacks—or tasted better.

We soon discovered the Western Steak House did much more than serve mammoth flapjacks. It also serves as the region's gathering spot for local folks to catch up on the latest news and gossip. All around us sat groups of three to five people, chatting, listening, observing, and enjoying one another's company.

One such group sat right next to us. Four elderly gentlemen, obviously longtime cronies, were commiserating at a rectangular table in the middle of the dining room. We didn't manage to get any of their names; they seemed far more interested in asking about us than in describing themselves, for when they saw Brian and me in our riding gear, they started in on us.

One said, "I made a commitment years ago never again to sweat." He looked like he'd kept that vow, too, with his belt on its last notch and his large sweet roll nearly eaten. A man next to him asked, through his well-trimmed mustache, "Doesn't perspiration make you miserable all day?" When I began to explain how the material in our shirts "breathes" well and that our riding shorts have padding that wicks away moisture, he said, "Stop! That's more than I want to know, especially over breakfast!"

We tried to turn the tables on them and asked them a little about themselves, but were left mostly in the dark. Not that we didn't get a response! The eldest of the men, an eighty-four-year-old retired farmer, told us all kinds of stories. He claimed that one of his friends raised armadillos and had managed to corner the market; that when we left Fredonia and headed east once more, it was all downhill from there; that he had been elected the town's police chief and that a friend was the mayor; that he retired in '84 and hadn't made a dime since, but instead lived off welfare. Most of the time as he held forth, the man across the table from him just sat in his chair, slowly shaking his head. The welfare comment must have taxed his patience, because he suddenly interrupted.

"Don't believe anything that man says," he warned us, pointing an accusing finger at his friend. "It's all a lie. He just likes to tell tall ones. I ain't no mayor and he ain't no police chief." As he continued to spill the beans, I looked at the accused, who was moving his index finger in a circle around his temple and pointing back to his tattletale friend. *Crazy, that one is.* It was his final, silent story.

Soon we took leave of these gentlemen, allowing them to sort out the troubled affairs of our troubled world. I thought, People everywhere would live longer and feel better if they took an occasional morning with good friends just to slow down and put their microwave lifestyles on simmer. Maybe we could solve the world's ills.

As we stepped into a chilly, mostly cloudy Kansas morning for another day's ride, I couldn't help but believe that these men were blessed with something precious, something that so much of America lacks today. How many of us have developed close, cherished friendships with men or women with whom we can have breakfast one morning when all of us shuffle into our eighties? How many of us can sit down in a particular place at a particular time and know that we'll find unconditional love and acceptance there—as well as a lot of mutual, good-natured sparring? How many of us spend enough time with the same people over many years to ensure that when we reach retirement age, we won't have to wonder whether anyone will remember us?

In my office in Colorado Springs is a Scrabble game box which I keep propped in the corner as a reminder of the great friend who gave it to me. There's also a picture of nine softball players taken on a grass and dirt field in Missouri one hot August afternoon. In the back row with broad shoulders and a winning smile is my Scrabble opponent. Joe White and I became good friends almost immediately when we first met in 1986. He was a broadcast guest on *Focus on the Family* and was as nervous as anyone I'd ever seen. He never looked up from his notes once during the entire interview. He later told me, "I was panicked and knew if I looked at you or Dr. Dobson, I'd probably freeze up." He did a wonderful job, but might as well have been in another room.

Joe and I have since become best friends and enjoy challenging each other to anything. We're both very competitive. Unfortunately, the only thing to date I've found I can consistently beat him at is Scrabble.

He and I know we can confide in one another and it'll stay private. We enjoy a trust that won't be broken. I wish we could meet frequently around a table similar to the one we stood by this morning and laugh and talk for a few hours. How therapeutic that would be!

There's a lot to be said for lifetime friendships built strong and solid through the course of family triumphs and personal tragedies, community emergencies and neighborhood celebrations. And I wonder: When I'm eighty-four, will I be able to look forward to leisurely breakfasts with a handful of my own cronies? Will I tell tall tales to visitors just passing through? Will my friends shake their heads at me and urge listeners to disregard my wild stories? Will I silently warn observers that my friends are really off their rockers?

I don't know. But I do know that I have about thirty-four years to continue doing what I can to develop and nurture such deep, soul-enriching friendships. All it takes is time, commitment, like-minded men or women, and a convenient, hospitable meeting place. If I can rustle up those priceless ingredients, then I can whip up friendships as big, sweet, and satisfying as the flapjacks with strawberries and whipped cream served at the Western Steak House in Fredonia, Kansas. And so can you.

The Dinosaur Not So National Park

Just outside Erie, Kansas, along Highway 400–47, we spotted a herd of dinosaurs. Really. A hulking Tyrannosaurus Rex, a grazing Apatosaurus, a pair of Velociraptors, a Stegosaurus, a perched Pterosaur, and even a Woolly Mammoth (the only mammal in the whole reptilian bunch). Green dinosaurs, red dinosaurs, blue dinosaurs, yellow dinosaurs (and the white mammoth)—who knew that prehistory was so colorful?

I pedaled over to the house to find someone to tell me if I was seeing things. A woman appeared at the door and directed me to the garage in back, where I was told I would find her husband hard at work on yet another long-dead dino.

We found Bob Dorris shrouded by sparks flying from his newest welding project. He was perhaps eighty years old and wore green slacks, a gray-checked cotton shirt, a brown hat with black band, and worn brown work boots. He'd packed his garage with all manner of treasure useful for assembling iron dinosaurs—old paint cans, stray wire, thick chains, spare car and truck parts (I'm not sure what kind of dinosaur could use the rusting wheelchair piled in back; maybe a *really* old one?). When Bob saw Brian and me pull up, he set his welder aside and kindly told us the story behind his metallic zoo.

"What are you working on?" I asked.

"To tell the truth, I'm not sure," he replied. "I had an idea which I began with, but now I'm not sure. I think I'll have to cut it apart and start again. Sometimes I restart several times before I get a clear idea of what I should do."

That struck me as very much like life in general!

Bob has been building dinosaurs for ten years. Whenever he decides it's time to bring to life one of these ancient brutes, he visits the Smithsonian Institution in Washington, D.C., making sure to take along his camera. He snaps some pictures of the creatures on display, then returns home with his "blueprints," setting to work in his garage with extinct vehicle parts not quite as ancient as the beasts they will mimic. Abandoned oil pans become dinosaur heads; pistons and camshafts serve as vertebrae; brakes turn into shoulders; fenders are slowly transformed into ribs. Bob makes regular trips to the junkyard at Chanute for parts. He tries to get his dinosaurs to look like those in his photos; if they don't, he starts over. His fifteen-foot-high T-Rex took him fifteen months to build; his twenty-foot-high, forty-foot-long Apatosaurus (often mistakenly called a Brontosaurus) was two years in the making.

Up till now, his dinosaurs have been for display only; now he wants one that his grandkids can play in and on. Such a dino will also come in handy when local schoolkids drop by on field trips, as they've been doing for several years.

Eventually we had to ask: Why does he do it? Does he have a consuming interest in these awesome monsters from the distant past? "Nope," Bob says, matter-of-factly. "I don't really know anything about dinosaurs. I just build them as a hobby." That word "hobby" is important to Bob; it also means his creations won't be showing up on the auction block any time soon. A few years back a wealthy businessman asked how much it would cost to take the residents of Bob's zoo home with him. Bob said they weren't for sale. The man pressed Bob to name his price; Bob repeated they weren't for sale. Today they continue to stand guard on the east side of the Dorris home, safely crouched or standing or stalking or perched around the unobtrusive little sign that proclaims, "Dinosaur Not So National Park."

Re-creating extinct beasts isn't the only hobby that consumes Bob's time these days. He's also a rock collector. His rock and mineral collection spreads over a good chunk of his property; the entire yard almost qualifies as a museum. If you strolled around the premises, I'm sure he could spend hours telling you what he has and where he got it. But perhaps his favorite rock is the one he carted around in the trunk of his car for several years. Decades ago he carried off a large slab of rock taken from ground zero of the first atomic bomb, exploded in the desert of New Mexico. Other souvenir-seeking military types had their pebble-sized glass chunks confiscated by superiors—but Bob still lays claim to his much heftier memento. And he never worried much about possible radiation poisoning. "I've raised a family and there still doesn't seem to be anything wrong with them," he explains.

It turns out that Bob and I have a couple of points of connection. First, he spent many years in the Air Force, working in California and elsewhere on research and development projects. He retired about the same time the F–16 fighter was introduced. My own dad worked at the famed "Skunk Works" in Palmdale, California—a formerly super-secret division of

Lockheed Martin that still develops exotic aircraft for clients such as the U.S. Air Force.

I was interested to learn about Bob's memories of Southern California, but he seemed more intent on discussing our recent trip through the rugged Arizona countryside. He was fascinated with our travels and especially with the Arizona desert. It became clear that he loved the area from Flagstaff up to Cortez. He'd traveled through it many times and had often vacationed there. He spent several wistful minutes reminiscing about long-ago stays in little, out-of-the way, next-to-nothing spots. He recalled one motel tucked up against the red mountains.

"It was called the Anastagi something or other," he said. Brian and I instantly remembered seeing the place, now abandoned. "It used to be a nice spot," Bob continued. "Its owners kept it open year around for the Hollywood crews who came out several times a year to shoot Westerns." He paused, as if carried back in time for a moment, then continued, "They needed a good place to stay and the owners could make enough money on the movie types alone to stay open year 'round." His voice cracked and he finished, "But those days have long passed."

Like many whom we met in our travels, Bob deeply envied our ability to take a month off and see the country. He desperately wished he could go with us, but that was impossible. With age often comes illness, and he and his wife were recovering from a nasty bout with the flu. Although the worst had passed a couple of months before, they still were dealing with the bug's energy-sapping effects. Bob wanted to get well enough to make one last trip to the desert. He longed to spend some time in that country he adored.

Not that he dislikes his present surroundings. Bob, who grew up in Fort Worth, Texas, has lived in Erie for twenty years. He moved there two decades ago to be with his parents when his mother became seriously ill. He bought this place by the side of the highway and has called it home ever since. Some time ago he adopted a dog named K.C., a beagle who "dropped in" from the highway. A previous dog (not K.C.) is the reason for a sign posted out front in big, black letters. The signs says,

"Bad dog," with small print below it explaining, "at least, he thinks he is." To be honest, I doubt K.C. thinks of himself as a bad dog at all. Walk anywhere near him and he'll instantly roll over on his back, imploring you to stroke his stomach. Not exactly vicious.

A far cry from some of the dinos skulking in Bob's yard, metallic jaws anxious to chomp and steel claws eager to pounce! I marvel when I see them ... and am mighty grateful they're extinct.

I doubt I'll ever again be able to look at dinosaur skeletons (or sculptures) without thinking of Bob Dorris. I'm glad to have met him, a resourceful man who served his country faithfully and is now serving his grandkids and local schoolboys and girls by firing their young imaginations with grand visions of gargantuan beasts gone the way of ... well, the dinosaurs.

Bob, I thank you for the tour. And I hope your kind *never* becomes extinct.

Saints in the Heartland

Take a quick quiz: Where did the first Christian martyr in North America lose his life?

If you answered "New England" or "California" or "Florida" or "Texas," take a seat at the back of the class. But if the name "Kansas" came to your lips, congratulations! For right here in the very heart of this country, way back in 1542— eighty years before the Pilgrims landed at Plymouth Rock—a Franciscan friar named Juan de Padilla was killed by the Indians he came to evangelize.

Surprised? Most folks are. They have little idea of how rich the Christian legacy of this nation is. Much has been said in the last few years about the religious heritage of America, and a fierce debate has raged over whether this country was founded as a Christian nation directed by Christian principles. While I don't intend to join the debate here, I do want to point out that a vast portion of this country *was* explored and settled by men and women with strong Christian convictions, spiritual trailblazers who brought their passionate Christian faith with them. Almost everywhere we pedaled across this great land we found markers and mementos and monuments commemorating the early pioneers who arrived and settled in remote areas precisely because they desired to live out their faith in Jesus Christ. The region around St. Paul, Kansas, is one such area.

The tiny town of St. Paul claims fewer than 700 citizens, yet it is the site for an enormous Catholic church which suddenly rises up from the prairie just off the highway. Travel just a bit down the road and you encounter the burned-out hulk of another large church, built in the mid–1800s. Nearby is a roadside memorial dedicated to Father Padilla and the Spanish explorer he originally accompanied, Francisco Vásquez de Coronado. An enormous stone cross erected in 1950 tells the story of Friar Padilla, while a historical marker briefly describes Coronado's early Kansas explorations.

Those memorials explain that while zeal for the Christian faith brought Juan de Padilla to the center of North America, it was gleaming visions of gold that seduced Coronado. An Indian called the Turk had told salivating Spaniards about the Kingdom of Quivira, where the trees were said to be hung with golden balls and whose people used pots and pans of beaten gold. The temptation created by these stories of boundless wealth proved too powerful to resist, and in 1541 Coronado handpicked thirty horsemen, set out from Texas, and followed his compass to what is now Kansas. Much to his dismay, his quest for gold turned up empty. The Turk found out how deep was that dismay when he confessed he had lied about the place; one night the angry Spaniards strangled him.

Still, Coronado liked the country he saw, calling it "the best I have ever seen for producing all the products of Spain." For twenty-five days in the summer of 1541 Coronado remained in the grass-hut villages of the Quiviran Indians, then left for New Mexico. Padilla went with him, but the following year he returned to Quivira as a missionary. Before the year was out, he was killed by the Indians, the first Christian martyr in the present United States.

Padilla's early missionary efforts were not wasted but helped to fuel later Christian outreach. In 1820 Osage Indians asked the Right Reverend William Louis DuBourg to send "Black Robes" (Jesuits) to them so that they might learn of the God of the Bible and of Jesus Christ, his Son. In response, the

Reverend Charles de la Croix was sent to the area on April 1, 1821. He visited the Osage along the Osage River in western Missouri and soon the Jesuits were given exclusive care of whites and the native Americans throughout the Missouri Valley. Twelve Jesuit missionaries joined the Reverend de la Croix on May 31, 1823, and in 1847 a Catholic mission for Osage Indians living along the Neosho and Verdigris Rivers was founded. The next year the first Catholic church in southern Kansas was built. Some have called the Osage Mission "the Antioch of the Nineteenth Century" because of the large number of missionary stations and churches that were established from the mission. In 1870 it was estimated that the missionaries ministered to 962 families, about 5,000 souls. After the Osage-ceded lands were opened up for homesteading, they formed a magnet that drew large numbers of early settlers to locate near the mission. The descendants of many of these early settlers still live on or near the old homesteads.

With churches also usually come schools, and that's what happened in St. Paul. A manual labor school for boys was established by the Jesuits, while a school for girls was founded by the Sisters of Loretto. On October 10, 1847, four Sisters of Loretto arrived at the mission and welcomed their first Osage girls within two hours of their own arrival. During the Civil War, when much other property was destroyed, the mission was always spared; school was never suspended. When the Osage moved to Indian Territory in 1870, white children replaced them. The schools became St. Francis Institute for Boys and St. Anne's Academy for girls. St. Francis closed in 1891; St. Anne's burned down in 1895 and was not rebuilt. The town, which had been known as Osage Mission, was renamed St. Paul that same year.

Could St. Paul, Kansas, teach us something about the debate concerning the Christian roots of our country? Perhaps—just perhaps—we do not make the most strategic use of our limited time and resources when we debate year after year whether the Founding Fathers desired this to be a Christian or a secular nation. Perhaps that's not the real question at all. Maybe the central lesson to be learned is not to be found in documents chronicling the official birth of the nation in

1776 but in considering the individual religious histories of hundreds of little towns and villages flung across the vastness of the continent—histories of passionate Christian faith that often precede by centuries the events leading up to the Revolutionary War.

When we choose such a tack, we quickly discover that the faith "once delivered to the saints" plays a far greater role in the founding and growth of this nation than many of us have imagined. Some cynics might object, "But would Friar Padilla have journeyed to the Quivira had Coronado not set out to find gold?" Perhaps not. But the fact is that when Coronado left, never to return, Padilla made the journey back one year later to spread the faith he loved. His martyr's death is a reminder still that the Christian faith is not ultimately a matter of debate, but of action. We would not be where we are without the dedication, persistence, and zeal of our forebears in the faith who dared to live out their Christianity. St. Paul, Kansas, reminds me of all of this. It also wordlessly asks a question: What lessons will my own faith teach those who come after me?

You see, it isn't enough to debate the Christian underpinnings of our country. It falls to us to live out the Christian faith so that our descendants will find a solid underpinning of faith for the future. That, it seems to me, is the real challenge.

CHAPTER 6

R & R in the Show Me State

We arrived in the Show Me State on Day 19 of our adventure, rolling hills and thick groves of trees telling us we had left the plains of Kansas behind. We ended that day at Highway 37 in Golden City, another of those little towns that dot the back roads of America. It boasts one main street with several blocks of small retail stores. The basics are available: groceries, shoes, insurance, gas, and at least one cafe. If you want to do some serious shopping, you have to drive to Springfield.

"Do you boys need to do that in the middle of the road?" a slightly perturbed motorist asked as we loaded our bikes into the van near the only stop sign in town.

"Sorry," Brian responded halfheartedly. I suppose the man was in a hurry to get somewhere. Even in Golden City, the affliction of time pressure persists.

The next morning, May 29, we were treated to scenes of the hilly, wooded Missouri countryside. In Ash Grove we stopped at Prentices and filled our plates and our stomachs with good food, all for $3.99 apiece.

As we pulled the bikes out of the van in the restaurant parking lot, a mechanic from the auto repair shop next door walked over. "One of you guys wouldn't be from *Focus on the Family*, would you?" he asked. It seems his brother-in-law had called and asked him to look for us. He asked all the usual questions and then volunteered, "I'm not the church-goin' one in the family, but I'd like to follow your trip on radio."

I used our cellular phone to call my office and get some station information for his area. There were a lot of options and he promised to tune in. I imagine somewhere a sister and brother-in-law were praying for this young man. Maybe you can join in, too.

By late afternoon we made it to Springfield, home of the Assemblies of God, where we were to stop at 5:30 P.M. for a reception at Northtown Mall. And what a reception! About seventy-five had gathered there to greet us and hear of the first twenty days of our adventure. I was absolutely shocked and delighted to receive a proclamation from the mayor of Springfield, the third largest city in Missouri, who along with a member of his city council honored these two cyclists from Colorado. Dr. Gordon Dutile from Southwestern Baptist University also was there; several years before the Dutiles had hosted Nancy and me when we spoke for the school's marriage weekend, and at that time I received an honorary doctorate in journalism.

Most of the folks who came out to greet us were listeners of *Focus on the Family*. As I spoke to the group, a big banner behind me welcomed us and emphasized my connection to *Focus*. Throughout our trip I was repeatedly struck by the love and admiration listeners have for the broadcast; the appreciation they expressed was simply overwhelming. The group in Springfield was no different. One woman brought us a basket filled with bread and fruit. A couple gave Brian a contribution for his charity. And once more I was deeply honored and thrilled that God would so bless the ministry with such loyal supporters. It is indeed a privilege to be associated with *Focus on the Family* and to be connected through it to the many millions of quality people who listen so faithfully.

When I think of all the people who go to work each day and dislike their job, I almost feel guilty. *Almost.* I have never had a greater sense of being in the Lord's will than I do at *Focus*. Every skill I ever learned has been pulled out and utilized in my years with the broadcast team. In some ways, my tenure with *Focus on the Family* bears a spiritual parallel to our bike trip. Before going to *Focus* I had done what most men and women in the media do: I'd jumped around, trying to climb the corporate ladder. Since starting at an FM station in Los Angeles in 1966, I'd held twelve jobs before walking through the doors at 41 East Foothill Boulevard in Arcadia on a summer afternoon in 1981. By then I was ready to settle down and persevere through any frustrations and difficulties. That same act of perseverance was what kept me on the bike; I knew I could finish if I just stayed with it. Then and now, it was time to stay the course.

Our Springfield reception also provided us with a grim and terrible reminder of the fragility of the family. One man in the audience distributed yellow, photocopied posters asking for information about his missing fifteen-year-old son. Andrew D. Owensby, along with seventeen-year-old Bradley M. Prater, had vanished without a trace. The poster showed reproduced photographs of the pair and said they were last known to be "traveling in 1981 Chevrolet van, medium brown with broken TV antenna on top; Missouri License #672-BZN. If seen, contact your local sheriff's department."

It is a horrible commentary on our times that child abduction is a large and growing menace in this country. Did you know that every year, more than 1 million children are reported missing? That's the figure supplied by the office of Juvenile Justice and Delinquency Prevention. It has been estimated that one child disappears in this land every eighteen seconds. A study by the U.S. Department of Justice said that in 1988 there were 354,000 children abducted by family members, 450,700 runaways, and 114,600 attempted abductions by non-family members. And perhaps even more chilling, it is estimated that 40,000 children under the age of seventeen are sold each year to pimps, sexual degenerates, and pornographers.

Since 1984, when it was established under a Congressional mandate, the National Center for Missing and Exploited Children has handled more than 1 million calls and has trained 138,000 law enforcement officials and other experts about the reality of child abduction. That agency alone has assisted in the recovery of 32,000 missing children since its inception. Yet that is a tiny percentage of the total number of abductees.

My heart went out to this father in Springfield. I pray that his son is well and healthy and that one day soon he will be returned to his family. I hope that someone spots a poster somewhere and connects it with the missing boy.

But let me take this opportunity to ask you a few questions. If you have minor children, have you drilled them on how to avoid possible abductors? Have you instructed them to be wary of strangers, to remember and act on the simple acronym SKY (Scream, Kick, Yell) if a stranger should try to force them to come with him or her? Have you reminded them to use the buddy system, to hang around groups of people as much as possible, to avoid running into open fields or wooded areas if pursued by strangers?

I took our little seven-year-old grandson to his first karate lesson the other night. What an interesting experience, watching kids who struggle with knowing which foot is their left and which is their right go through a series of commands from their dojo. Legs were flailing everywhere. I was interested to learn that the boys and girls were not instructed to summon assistance against an attacker by yelling "help." Apparently, most people don't respond to a plea for help because they don't want to get involved. But if a child yells "fire!" everyone comes running. There are two sad social commentaries here: First, that our apathetic society does not want to assist a stranger; and second, that our children must be taught self-preservation at such an early age.

There is so much more that our children should know regarding the dangers of child abduction; have you begun their training in this crucial area? I admit it isn't a pleasant topic to think about. But surely it would be much worse to distribute a photocopied poster asking readers for information on the whereabouts of a child whose photo came out of your own family album.

The end of Day 20 brought more than the promise of another night's sleep. We were exhausted by this point in our trip—in large measure because we hadn't yet taken a full day off—and the wear and tear was beginning to show. For the last several days Brian had been complaining about pain in the back of his knee. Despite taking several ibuprofen tablets each morning before beginning to ride, his leg began to throb after a few hours. I wasn't having any knee problems, but I sure needed the rest. I felt as if I'd been up several nights in a row, cramming for exams. Every fiber in my body was exhausted.

In my first radio job, I worked the overnight shift and had a hard time sleeping during the day. I would catch up on the weekends, but by Wednesday I was wrung out. I can remember driving home in morning rush hour traffic, slapping myself to stay awake. More times than I want to recall, while behind the wheel I would jerk to an awareness that I didn't remember the last several miles. I must have been in some pre-sleep stupor. I'm amazed I never had an accident.

I was fast approaching that same level of fatigue as we pushed on toward Virginia Beach, Virginia, and I knew it wasn't good. That's why we had scheduled two days off. Brian would use most of that time to return to Colorado Springs to attend his brother's high school graduation while I would rest, work on our bikes, do laundry, and enjoy the company of my hosts.

And Missouri surely is not a bad place to rest. The state boasts 902,000 acres of waterways and more than 50,000 miles of rivers and streams, with nearly 200 species of fish living in those waters, more than any other state. Missouri also has more free-flowing streams, more springs, and more types of wild-flowers than any other state. If you're into spelunking (which we weren't), you should know it is home to more than 5,000 known caves, twenty-four of which offer guided tours.[1] And don't worry too much if you can't recall whether you're supposed to pronounce the state's name as MissourEE or MissourAH. A debate on that topic has been raging since the 1800s and has yet to be resolved.[2] So just relax and enjoy yourself.

A day after the Springfield reception, it was time for another phone interview with my boss, Dr. James Dobson:

Interview Three

Dobson: Mike, ... how's the pedaler doing these days?

Trout: Boy, you ought to see these legs! They've never looked so good.

Dobson: I've never been interested in your legs! Where are you?

Trout: We've been through Kansas. We stayed in El Dorado, we stayed in Fredonia, we headed through Pittsburg, Kansas, across the border into Missouri. We were in Springfield yesterday and now we're going up and down the hills of the Ozarks.

Dobson: Now, the mayor of Springfield kind of hosted you?

Trout: We had a marvelous meeting yesterday in a mall in Springfield. Radio stations were there; we had three or four radio stations and interviews and a wonderful crowd. I'm telling you, I'm just blown away. I can't believe that people would care that I'm coming through town on a bicycle. Of course, it's because they've been touched by *Focus on the Family*.

Dobson: It's my understanding, Mike, that people are continuing to come out and greet you, ride along with you, hold up banners, wave at you, hand you water. Even serve you dinner.

Trout: They really are. We have had just one marvelous experience after another where people have stood out on the side of the road, holding up big banners saying, "Welcome, Mike Trout," "Welcome, Focus on the Family," and folks have been along the side of the road, shaking hands. We've been invited into people's homes and we've eaten dinners and lunches at churches. It's just been amazing how people have honored us.

Dobson: You called me Monday night to say that a church had invited you in, people gathered around and fixed a dinner for you?

Trout: That's happened several times. I think I was in El Dorado, Kansas, when I spoke with you. We were at the First Baptist Church. It was so nice because we laughed a lot. We have been on these bikes—you know, you just put your head down and you pedal a hundred and a hundred and twenty miles or whatever it might be, and you're bone tired and all you can think about for the last hour and a half is that hot shower that looms ahead somewhere in some motel. And we sat around the table, about thirty or forty people, and they had fixed a potluck dinner on Memorial Day night—I couldn't believe *that*—and we just laughed.

Dobson: You spend ten hours a day on a bicycle seat—you have to laugh a lot, don't you? Either that or cry, I think. You're still enjoying it, though?

Trout: I am. It really has been nice. And as I said earlier, it's been especially meaningful to have people honor us as they open up their homes and open up their hearts. We've talked to some folks in restaurants. A person wheeling in on a bicycle is pretty unintimidating, and so they tend to talk to you a lot. One lady just the other day came up to our table and asked where we were from. "Oh, I know Colorado Springs!" she said. "Focus on the Family is up there. Do you know Focus?" And I said, "Absolutely." Time and time again, it's amazing how your books and the outreach of the ministry has touched so many people in so many different places. And I also must say that our radio stations through these areas have been just marvelous as they have lined things up for us. I met with folks in a Wal-Mart parking lot at lunchtime yesterday and we had a great time, then went and got something to eat. The radio stations have just been very, very cooperative.

Dobson: People are so friendly. I was in Nordstrom's last night, a department store, and bought a tie. I gave a credit card to the salesman and he looked at it and he looked at me, looked back at that credit card and said, "Come here." I didn't know what he was wanting me to do. He brought me around behind the counter, dialed his home phone and his wife picked up the phone, and he handed the phone to me. I'm talking to his wife all of a sudden!

Trout: Well, everybody says to say "hello" to Dr. Dobson when I go through the towns and see them. It's fun! It's kind of like Charles Kuralt on the road. Except we're on the bikes.

Dobson: And the bike is still functioning, right?

> **Trout:** Absolutely!
> **Dobson:** And you're riding about a hundred miles a day?
> **Trout:** A little over, yes.
> **Dobson:** That's incredible!
> **Trout:** Look for two guys on red and yellow bikes. And give us a wide berth when you go by.
> **Dobson:** And one of 'em's white around the mouth!
> **Trout:** That's right!
> **Dobson:** Thanks, Mike, it's always fun to talk to you. We sure do miss you here and we'll check in again.

Finally, a Couple Days Off

We took a whirlwind trip down to Camps Kanakuk and Kanakomo, about forty miles south of Springfield, to speak with two groups of counselors working with young campers there. I serve on the board of the nonprofit camp Kids Across America, and it was good to reconnect in person with the staff there. We arrived late, gave a brief presentation, then motored back to our accommodations for the night—a delightful evening with Spike and Darnel White.

Spike and Darnel are the parents of Joe White, the force behind Kanakuk and Kanakomo, the largest group of Christian sports camps in the country. Spike really is the grandfather of those camps although they were in operation before he purchased them. At the time the camps were barely chugging along, but he roared into town and breathed life into them.

Both Spike and Darnel are extraordinary individuals. Both in their 80s, they remain remarkably active. How many people do you know who take up kayaking at age seventy? Yet that's what Spike did. Although he has undergone heart bypass surgery, he continues to exercise like crazy and to seek out unusual activities. He has a mind like a steel trap and remembers everything.

This amazing pair demonstrate how an active lifestyle can keep a person healthy and involved with life. The Whites also represent the "graying of America" and are examples of how our pictures of the elderly are rapidly changing.

I vividly remember sitting in the living room several years ago of then Surgeon General C. Everett Koop and hearing him talk about what he dubbed "the squaring of the population pyramid." "We are less than ten years away from a demographic phenomenon," he said.

He meant that senior citizens would then equal or outnumber the "kids" in the younger categories. That population shift will bring unprecedented problems and opportunities. Never before will a nation have at its disposal such a preponderance of experience and wisdom (I'll be in the experience group). And I don't believe it's coincidental that euthanasia legislation is on the ballot everywhere. Satan is at work as never before!

Today more men and women are living longer than in any other time in the nation's history, and they're more active than ever. Life expectancy in this country is steadily rising, and many experts predict that boys and girls born at the turn of this century can expect to live at least one hundred years.

One of the most powerful lobbies on Capitol Hill these days is the American Association of Retired Persons, a "nonprofit, nonpartisan organization dedicated to helping older Americans achieve lives of independence, dignity and purpose." It claims a membership of thirty-three million. And those numbers will surely rise. The oldest members of the Baby Boom generation already have or are just now turning fifty (I'm one of them!). There's even a National Association of Baby Boomers dedicated to serving the needs of the seventy-eight million Americans who were born between 1946 and 1964.

According to *American Demographics* magazine, these Americans are characterized by much more than huge numbers. "Baby boomers are entirely unlike older generations of Americans, both in attitudes and lifestyles," wrote Cheryl Russell in 1995. "Boomers are a well-educated generation. This makes them more demanding and sophisticated consumers than people in the current mature market. Boomers are also highly individualistic, which makes them independent and self-indulgent. . . . Sales of skin creams, suntan lotions, hair coloring, cosmetics, vitamins, and nutritional supplements are surging as millions of boomers join the battle against aging. Self-help books have become so popular that the *New York*

Times publishes a separate best-seller list for them. Spirituality, if not traditional religion, is seeing a rebirth as the burgeoning middle-aged population searches for life's meaning."[3]

I'm glad to say that Spike and Darnel already have this last issue nailed down. They are committed followers of Christ who continue to serve him in an amazing number of ways. They inspire me like few others do.

I recall a story Dr. Dobson told on a broadcast many years ago. I identified with it then and do even more so today. An elderly woman was asked what she thought about turning ninety. "I don't like it," she said. "I'm a prisoner in my own body." She was frustrated that she couldn't do physically what her mind was ready for. "I'm a twenty-six-year-old inside this aging frame," she insisted.

I'm already experiencing some of those same feelings. I feel like a thirty-five-year-old with sore shoulders! The heart scare I had before my trip across America was a wake-up call. I don't want to get to the home stretch and spend my remaining time on the sidelines because of irresponsible habits during these midlife years. My shoulders may hurt, but I don't have to let the rest of my body join them. Not quite yet, anyway.

After taking Brian to the airport, Ted and I headed up to the Lake of the Ozarks to stay with some good friends, Dick and Sherley Bott, who in my book are the ultimate hosts.

The Botts own radio stations throughout Missouri and Kansas and have others in Indiana, Oklahoma, California, and Tennessee. They continue to add more stations, the newest in Nebraska. Dick conducted about a dozen radio interviews with me by phone during our jaunt across the country and was the only one to connect with me while I was standing in the Atlantic Ocean at the end of the trip. But that's a tale for later.

One of the most moving stories I heard on my cross-country adventure came from Dick. A little more than a year ago his daughter Arla gave birth to a baby girl who was far from healthy. Months before Arla delivered, doctors told her that her baby had a fatal chromosome deficiency. The baby could not survive, they said, and they strongly recommended that Arla get an abortion.

Arla and her husband, Nick Eicher, managing editor with *World* magazine, are strongly pro-life and rejected the medical world's recommendation. They recognized the certainty of their daughter's death, but they refused to ignore their deep convictions regarding the sanctity of life. Their infant daughter lived for only three months, then died. No doubt those were the most painful weeks in the Eichers' lives. Yet those three months, as difficult as they were, gave Arla and Nick an opportunity to love their daughter, to hold her, to know her—and then to release her. The episode was deeply sad but also very complete. Rather than terminating the pregnancy early, the Eichers welcomed their daughter into the world and then, with hearts full of both sorrow and gratitude, all too soon bid her a tearful farewell. It's a gripping story, one that reminds me that while faithfulness to God isn't always easy, it is always the most rewarding choice.

The previous summer, our family was glued to the television, watching the Olympic games. Our youngest daughter, Meredith, has been involved in gymnastics since age four, when she almost memorized the TV movie about the Romanian phenom Nadia Comaneci. When we moved to Colorado Springs in 1991, Meredith began training at a wonderful gym called Aerials. Tom and Lori Forester own the facility and for a time in 1995 and 1996 coached a talented young Olympian named Keri Strugg.

Anyone who watched the vault competition in the '96 gymnastics finals will never forget the look of pain on Keri's face as she planted her feet on the winning leap. A badly sprained ankle had left her questionable as a competitor, but the team had needed her if the U.S. was to have a chance at the overall Gold Medal. As Keri hopped away on one leg after a near-perfect finish and tears poured down her chalk-covered cheeks, the nation crowned her a hero. She had pushed through excruciating physical and emotional pain to success.

Meanwhile, several hundred miles to the north, the Eichers endured a different type of pain. For them there would be no newspaper articles written about them, no television interviews, no magazine covers—but they are heroes nonetheless.

On the Road Again

On June 1 Brian rejoined us and we took off on one of the longest rides of our biking adventure. We rode from Springfield to Winona, a trip of nearly 125 miles. At the end of a largely uneventful day, we were invited to stay with the Peters family at the River's Edge Inn in Eminence, Missouri.

Lynett Peters is not a regular listener to *Focus on the Family,* but she does receive the magazine and saw an article in the May edition announcing my trip. She called my office and invited us to stay a night at their inn.

She and her husband, Alan, have three daughters. The age separation between their girls is almost identical to those of my own trio, although Nancy's and my daughters preceded theirs by about a decade. The Peters family had lived in Newton, Kansas—a town we biked through—but with a population of 16,700, the community was too large for their tastes and they sought out a smaller town. They are outdoor people, naturalists and environmentalists, and after vacationing in the Eminence area (population 582), decided the lifestyle there was more to their liking.

But would the girls get bored in such a little town? No, say the girls. One daughter is very involved in sports and the other two find plenty of activities elsewhere, including church camps. All three seem quite content with life in Eminence. One accommodation that the Peters family did have to make in moving to the area is that Mom and Dad go to one church, while the girls attend another with a stronger youth program. I wonder how common that is. My own family has switched churches in the past, not because of anything lacking for the adults but because the new church offered more for our kids. Because we were concerned about our kids and wanted them to get involved in church, we made a switch. Alan and Lynett Peters have worked out a similar solution.

The River's Edge Inn sits on the bank of Jack's Fork River, one of the cleanest rivers in the United States. You could step into a boat moored right outside your room, weigh anchor, and cruise all the way to the Gulf of Mexico. The area is an outdoorsman's paradise and provides some of the prettiest scenery anywhere.

All is not paradise in Shannon County where Eminence is located, however. Shannon is the poorest county in the state and one of the poorest in the nation. As the country's welfare system changes, a lot of Shannon County folks are going to have to figure out what to do—they'll have to find a way to earn more money. Yet, according to Lynett, some residents are ignoring opportunities that already exist. "I have a difficult time finding enough workers willing to help clean the Inn's rooms," she said. "Too many folks would rather not work because they say they can make more money on welfare." But with welfare program changes surely coming down the pike, that'll have to change. "The town is slowly dying," Lynett told me. "If it weren't for logging and tourists, we'd all dry up and blow away."

Alan described the inn as it was before the family purchased it nearly ten years earlier. "We've added the cabins where you're staying and cleaned up some of the waterfront," he said. The family obviously loves its retreat beside the river. They're here for the duration. They represent millions of other "grassroots" Americans who are living out their dreams in a spot of their own choosing beside a little ribbon of highway close to somewhere. Their middle daughter broke in on my thoughts with, "We like going to the Wal-Mart in Poplar Bluff." Everyone agreed and I imagined how simple and enjoyable life could be when the choices are few.

We were invited to dine on the delicious remnants of a barbecue the Peterses had served earlier that night for a group of twenty-one friends, then stayed up and talked till late. When we finally hit the sack for a good night's sleep, the gentle gurgling of the river provided a natural symphony perfect for sweeping us into dreamland. I'm not sure, but I may have dreamed of the Atlantic Ocean. After all, it was getting closer all the time.

The East Beckons

June 2 began with drizzle, but the road headed east and beckoned us on. We rode the hills through gorgeous country, some of the prettiest in the state. Brian, riding twenty feet ahead of me, was the first to hit rough road. As we crossed the county line, suddenly the maintenance—or lack thereof—changed dramatically. The sign announcing the county name indicated this was "Home of the Democrats." I wonder if the roads are paved only in election years?

By the end of the day we had cycled into and then out of Poplar Bluff, ending a little beyond in Fisk. The van picked us up and took us back into town, where a local church had provided accommodations for us at the Holiday Inn. The church sponsors the one-hour weekly broadcast that Focus on the Family produces for secular stations. In Poplar Bluff, that station is KWOC.

Focus on the Family produces a number of programs created specifically for secular stations, and we've been thrilled at the positive response to our kind of programming. I doubt it would have occurred ten or even five years ago. Today there seems to be an enormous openness to discussions of family issues. One indicator of this change is the popularity of personalities such as Dr. Laura Schlessinger, a certified marriage and family therapist who has her own radio program and is the author of a newspaper column as well as several books. Dr. Laura champions a conservative, pro-family message—even though her background sometimes prompts her to use language you'd never find on a Christian station—that has paved the way for dozens of other popular talk show hosts. Our own secular features began with a ninety second commentary in 1991.

During a recent phone conversation with the news director at a major radio station in Detroit, I was told, "Our listeners are saying they want more news and information that helps them at home." Now, that could mean almost anything, even weather and traffic, but he went on to say, "Our surveys are telling us the listener is anxious for help with their family. Marriages are stressed and the kids are in open rebellion." Apparently the need for basic, traditional, straightforward instruction is great.

The local Christian station in Poplar Bluff put on a marvelous meal for us outside its facility, erecting a tent to shelter both visitors and all the goodies various supporters had donated. All that evening folks stopped by to say "Hi!" We talked with them for a long time. Eventually I did a little interview at the station, which plays a lot of Southern Gospel. It is very proud to play music by local artists—"The Home Spun Hour," each Monday from 8 to 9 P.M., followed by *Focus on the Family*—who can be heard only in that area.

The station also seemed to be a rallying center for area churches. A number of pastors attended the reception and we had a wonderful time hearing from them. I was especially encouraged by the scores of listeners who turned out to express their love for the ministry of *Focus on the Family*. It's always good to know that your work is appreciated.

Hey, Waiter, Toss Me a Roll!

Overlooking Poplar Bluff is the First Baptist Church, an expanding congregation with a big brick building and a massive spire. When members and visitors leave its parking lot on Sunday morning, they see this sign: "You are entering the mission field."

I know a lot of churches have similar signs and I know the message they proclaim is true. Yet I wonder how often we live according to that truth? When I go to the grocery store, do I think of it as an opportunity to represent Christ to those who may not know him yet? When I get my hair cut, do I remember that flashing scissors and falling hair may be no more than incidental to God's plan for me that day? Do I realize that his real agenda may be that I present my barber with the claims of Jesus? How seriously do I take the truth that when I leave church services on Sunday morning, in reality I am entering the mission field?

Those are hard questions for 8:30 A.M. on a dismal June day when the sun hides behind stubborn fog and the temperature hovers somewhere in the mid-fifties. Still, they need to be answered … by all of us. But on June 3 I needed to mount my bike and head toward Dexter, where on an overpass we would meet with a program director and sales manager from KSIM as well as with a Nazarene pastor–insurance salesman who wanted to pray with us.

An hour later we arrived at our exit and learned the sales manager wanted to ride with us on his rusty mountain bike.

He said he'd been preparing for the ride, but after a few miles the hills and the traffic proved too much for him and his program director picked him up before we'd gone ten miles.

Soon our road conditions deteriorated markedly. The shoulder disappeared and traffic grew heavy. Brian had been praying that we would find an alternate route, and when we stopped at an intersection I approached a vehicle halted at the stop sign.

"Is there any other way to get to Sikeston?" I asked the driver. "We need to get to Lambert's Cafe."

"Oh, yeah," he replied. "A half a mile down the road you can take a side road that goes straight to where you need to be."

Seldom have I received a more immediate, practical answer to prayer! Prayer was our not-so-secret weapon throughout this trip. Sure enough, the road was right where we had been told and we wove safely through a few small towns until we reached our destination: Lambert's Cafe, "Only Home of Throwed Rolls."

The Lambert's in Sikeston is one of three restaurants in a small chain. Years ago Norm Lambert was a cook who decided to attract customers by baking fresh rolls and handing them out to patrons sitting at his counter. As business expanded, he added some tables and found the best way to get his rolls to customers was to toss them.

A news crew from ABC stopped in one day to have lunch at the restaurant and found the "throwed rolls" a fascinating story. The crew filmed buns flying through the air to waiting customers, and the next thing anyone knew, the place was nationally famous.

The tradition continues today. Waiters wander around the restaurant, throwing home-baked rolls just out of the oven at any customer who calls for one by raising a hand. And don't worry if you miss; another will fly by shortly. Other servers bring around large pots of fried okra, fried potatoes, black-eyed peas, macaroni and stewed tomatoes, and sorghum. Obviously, it's all you can eat.

The decor is interesting, too. State flags are tacked to the walls along with selected license plates from around the nation. Long booths, almost pew style, fill the middle part of the dining room, while on either side more traditional booths sit under sloped metal roofs, giving the place a "country" appearance. Dozens of nine-inch-long model airplanes made out of pop cans (mostly biplanes) hang from the ceiling.

Yet an undercurrent of tragedy flows just below the festive atmosphere. One of Norm's sons died at age twenty-one in an accident, and Norm could never quite come to grips with the loss. He had worked hard all his life, but the satisfaction of a job well done could not counterbalance the blinding grief. His family fell apart. His wife eventually left him and he subsequently committed suicide. His other sons now run the company and continue things just as their dad had set them up, but Norm's no longer around to enjoy their success.

That's the only thing I regret from my visit to Sikeston's marvelous Home of Throwed Rolls. The great food fueled our trip all the way to Paducah, Kentucky. I just wish I could have told Norm.

CHAPTER 7

Where Will You Spend Eternity— Smoking or Nonsmoking?

It's amazing to me how widespread some version of a "Southern accent" is. We started to hear its pleasant drawl in Kansas and noted it getting stronger and deeper and slower as we moved east and south. And when we crossed the Mississippi and Ohio Rivers on Day 23 of our journey, passing through the bottom tip of Illinois and entering Kentucky, we soon knew we were getting much closer to the wellspring of the gracious inflections and rhythms of the accent I call "Southern." When one of our team (I won't tell you which one) tried to speak with an elderly woman from Pembroke, Kentucky, her accent completely befuddled him; he needed a "translator" to get the message.

We knew we were entering the South in other ways, too. One of the most significant from my perspective was to note the region's spiritual passion as reflected in signs and markers along the way. In Paducah, Kentucky, for example—our first official stop east of the Mississippi—we read a sign that startled us not only for its message but also for its location. You must understand, where I come from it is uncommon to read religious messages on, let's say, a BP gas station marquee. I'm used to seeing messages there like, "Unleaded $1.47⁹." But at

155

a station in Paducah, the sign read, "Christ died for you—what have you done for him?"

Different, but I liked it.

We would continue to see such welcome signs throughout our few days in Kentucky, Tennessee, and North Carolina. On a water tower at the junction of highways 80 and 68, just before the Land Between the Lakes, we read the message, "Christ Above All." Outside of Rockwood, Tennessee, we passed a weathered stone cross with the carved inscription, "Nothing but the blood." In North Carolina we scanned a sign painted in red, yellow, and black depicting the fires of hell and warning readers to remember the coming eternal judgment. We saw billboards encouraging people to read the Bible and to go to church and to pray. But perhaps my favorite sign was a portable message board erected in front of a church that asked with both humor and gravity, "Where Will You Spend Eternity—Smoking or Nonsmoking?"

I'll take nonsmoking, please.

Our motel rooms in Paducah were paid for by the First Baptist Church and we were treated to dinner by Larry Richards at Pizza Inn, where a dozen or so people had gathered to welcome us to Kentucky. John Dalton from WCGF-FM conducted an informal interview with our team and we enjoyed another terrific evening with a wonderful group of people.

Gina Kunkerson told us she had mentioned our planned visit to her Sunday school class and they decided right then and there to take up an offering for us. It was that money which they used to pay for our lodging.

"Some of the members from our class were supposed to be here," she said. "I don't want to be the only one to report back next Sunday on your visit."

"I wish I could stay until then and thank them all in person," I replied.

If there was one thing I was enjoying, it was talking about our adventure. The trip was becoming everything I had hoped. Someone once said, "God created everything except experience." We live in a day when so many experiences are vicarious! We're one big spectator society, living out our dreams through the success and hard work of a few. It's staggering to contemplate the amount of time people sit in front of a television, watching someone else cook, golf, climb, fish, build, or what-have-you. I didn't want to talk about what someone else did. I wanted to make it personal.

Before leaving on this trip I had talked about my plans on the radio, partly to encourage others. I later received a letter from June Newman in Wisconsin who wrote, "It was you, Mike, who gave me the impetus to run a 4.6 mile race. I am sixty-one years old and have run the race in the past. I thought of running it again, but found reasons why I couldn't. After hearing you tell of your determination to finish your course, I thought, *Why not?* And guess what? I won for my age group! I felt great to be able to finish the race . . . but to come in first!" Then she added a big surprise: "I'm sending along my medal as I feel I would like you to have it! I wouldn't have run the race without you!"

As I hold that piece of bronze and ribbon, I can imagine why June made the decision to compete. The preparation and prayer that went into her effort, as well as the incredible experience of competing and winning, will never be forgotten. Whether we're nine or ninety, we can learn from the profound question asked by legendary baseball pitcher Satchel Paige, who wondered, "How old would you be if you didn't know how old you was?" Satch kept on pitching (and striking out younger players) long after his contemporaries had hung up their cleats and sagged into a sedentary lifestyle.

This country was made great and continues to be sustained by doers, not watchers!

We learned about one such doer as we rode through Paducah, a town that is now struggling with a senseless shooting. Paducah is located at the confluence of the Ohio and Tennessee rivers and is filled with large, gracious, even stunning homes that lend the city a quiet elegance. It is the only major city in the Commonwealth of Kentucky with an Indian name—from the Padouca Indians, once the largest tribe in the region. Local folklore speaks of the legendary Chief Paduke, a peaceful leader of a Chickasaw subtribe that hunted in the area. Churches, BIG churches, are everywhere and many have "historical interest" plaques erected on their front lawns. In fact, Paducah has more historic markers than any other Kentucky city.

Paducah's most influential citizen in the past century was no doubt Alben W. Barkley, who lived from 1877–1956. Barkley was a U.S. Representative from 1913–1927 and a U.S. Senator from 1927–1949 and 1954–1956. From 1937–1947 he served as Senate Majority Leader, where he was considered instrumental in securing passage of President Franklin D. Roosevelt's New Deal legislation. Barkley also was elected Vice President of the United States in Harry Truman's second administration from 1949–1953.

By any standard, that's quite a record of achievement! Yet Barkley himself apparently did not consider his accomplishments especially noteworthy. While speaking in Lexington, Virginia, in 1956, he suffered a massive heart attack and died. And his last words? "I would rather be a servant in the house of the Lord than sit in the seats of the mighty."

The morning of June 4 dawned overcast and damp, which didn't help the bad cold Brian had caught. Ignoring the discomfort, we mounted the bikes and pointed ourselves toward the Land Between the Lakes, a 170,000-acre reserve maintained by the Tennessee Valley Authority as a National Recreation Area. Its 300 miles of undeveloped shoreline mark off a unique area called "the heartland's outdoor playground." Stretching forty miles between Kentucky and Barkley Lakes, it offers camping, hunting, fishing, mountain biking, horseback trails, 2,500 acres set aside for all-terrain vehicles, a 750-acre Elk and Bison Prairie, a working nineteenth-century farm called The Homeplace, the Golden Pond Planetarium and Observatory, The Nature Station, and The Learning Center. At Golden Pond visitors can take in an exhibit on moonshiners, complete with a homemade still.

History is big here and historical markers are common. Many of them describe some aspect of the Civil War. One such marker reads, "Civil War Sniper. In 1862, Jack Hinson swore revenge against the union army when two sons were executed as bushwhackers. From ambush, he picked off men in blue uniforms on gunboats and on land. With a price on his head, he continued his vendetta until his gun bore 36 notches at close of war. He guided general Nathan B. Forest in his last campaign in area October to November, 1864."

Thankfully, visitors from the North these days don't have to worry about Confederate snipers. They're much more likely to encounter posters such as the one we saw advertising a Southern Gospel music concert. "Chuck Brand's Songs for the Soul with Preacher Man (Rev. Dale Boyd)" proclaimed the poster, which then encouraged visitors near Aurora to "take a break from fishing and come join in on the local fun of praising our Lord with ministering and song. Bring your lawn chairs."

And no sniping allowed.

After riding eighty-five miles, Brian and I were more than ready to end the day in Hopkinsville. As we pulled into the motel, we noticed a white pickup with a slender young man inside. He studied us for a while, got out of his truck, and said to me softly, "Are you Mike Trout?"

It turned out he was an avid listener to *Focus on the Family.* He happened to be taking dinner to his wife, who was working that evening, and he thought he might have seen us on the side of the road. He had no agenda other than to greet us. We learned he had been a coal miner until age twenty, then went back to school. Today he is an occupational therapist at a local nursing home. He had only a few minutes to spare and he wanted to spend them wishing us well. Who says people are colder, less trusting, less appreciative? The more we pedaled, the more my faith in the average American increased.

We didn't explore much of Hopkinsville, which seems as tired as Paducah is lively. It looks to be much more blue-collar and wilted than its neighbor to the northwest. Yet "tired" doesn't mean "inactive" and looks can be deceiving. At one edge of town stands a memorial honoring 248 soldiers based out of Fort Campbell, who died in Newfoundland on December 12, 1985, upon their return from a multinational peacekeeping mission in the Sinai. The Fort Campbell Memorial Park reminds visitors that Hopkinsville has a proud history, one which its citizens are careful to remember. A sense of history like this is just the kind of thing that can keep us going when we'd rather throw in the towel.

I've always liked the phrase, "When the going gets tough, the tough get going." That's the same sentiment that pushed Patrick Henry to declare in 1965, "Give me liberty or give me death." That kind of fervor also prompted English cyclist Tommy Simpson to breathlessly plead with spectators who came to his aid to "Put me back on my bike" when he collapsed while climbing one of the most grueling hills in the 1967 Tour de France. Less than half a mile later Simpson wobbled once more, then dropped to the pavement, never to regain consciousness. His death shocked the racing world and his last words are known by every professional cyclist today.

Brian and I weren't considering throwing in the towel on our own journey quite yet, but we were tired. The Atlantic Ocean was still more than a week away and the Appalachians were out there somewhere. But when we remembered that the Pacific was more than three times that far away—and the Rockies had been conquered—we were encouraged by our own recent accomplishments. We just needed to keep plugging along.

Our evening was again filled with the pleasant company of new friends who sought us out to learn about our journey. We were treated to dinner by Jim Adams, the general manager of local radio station WNKJ (The World Needs King Jesus). After a filling meal at one of the two Chinese restaurants in town, we drove to the station for a tour and interview. A former church facility provided the perfect location for WNKJ. The sanctuary is used for live broadcasts and the Sunday school classrooms have been transformed into studios and control rooms. The former church is in an inner-city neighborhood; the congregation long ago moved to the suburbs.

As we were leaving for our motel, Jim's wife pulled up in the parking lot with a station wagon filled with young girls. They had been attending a local youth group and she was chauffeuring them home. I was moved by her simple act of service toward these children who need adult role models. After a hurried introduction and visit, the carload of preteens was off into the night once more. For the Adamses, sharing Jesus with the world starts in their own neighborhood. And that's just as it should be.

Getting Closer

Determination is essential when you wake up to yet one more day of overcast skies and light rain. Those were the dreary conditions as we left Hopkinsville. We passed through Trenton, briefly crossing the infamous "Trail of Tears," a route marking the forced migration of Indians to a reservation west of the Mississippi in which thousands died. Soon Kentucky receded behind us and Tennessee lay beneath our tires. We immediately noticed an improvement in the road, with a newly resurfaced blacktop and a shoulder a foot and a half wide. The wind kicked up and we tried drafting behind the van, but the increased traffic in the East makes drafting difficult, if not impossible. We weren't in Kansas anymore, Toto.

Along this same route, more than forty years ago, my parents, two sisters, and I would drive each summer. During one of our vacation races along what we now call "the back roads," an event took place which is forever imprinted in my memory.

We had come to the end of another long day in the car and sought food and rest in a small Tennessee town. After moving our bags from the car to a pleasant motel room, we walked to a nearby cafe, one of those restaurants you saw by the thousands in towns and cities everywhere—counter seating for perhaps a dozen customers, with tables accommodating maybe another twenty-five. The menu was heavy on fried food and featured at least three main dinner dishes with mashed potatoes and gravy, plus green beans or succotash (lima beans, corn, and tomatoes cooked together). As we seated ourselves at a table, a black man of about sixty walked in and up to the counter. He was about to sit down when one of the two waitresses said she was sorry, but he would have to go back outside and around to a window in the rear if he wanted to order food. He left without complaint ... but my dad was incensed. This kind of discrimination may have been commonplace in Tennessee, but we hadn't experienced it on the West Coast.

As swiftly as we settled in, we stood and left, letting the staff know that we weren't going to support a place that had two sets of standards for their customers, based solely upon the color of their skin. I couldn't have been more than seven or eight at the time, but my own feelings about equality and human worth were forever molded in that moment.

I wish all of us as parents could see instantly the impressions we make on young lives as we act and react throughout each day. Dr. Dobson calls these "teachable moments," and they're occurring constantly. The trick is to take advantage of them while they're still "moments" and before they become "history." Race is still a troubling issue in our country. Can you think of ways you have shaped your children's attitudes about people who are different than you? And are you satisfied with what you taught?

A Chameleon or a Weasel?

In Springfield (that's Tennessee, not Missouri) singer Steve Chapman picked us up at the first stoplight in town to take us to lunch at his home outside Nashville. Steve and his wife, Annie, are longtime friends. I first met them about a dozen years ago when they sang at a chapel service for Focus on the Family. From that moment on we fell in love with them as a couple and with their music and with their kids.

I don't know that I have ever met a couple who have done a better job with their children than have Steve and Annie Chapman. Their son and daughter both seem to have grown up very healthy and with a deep love for the Lord. They have a desire to minister, are respectful of their parents, and treat others courteously. I'm sure Steve and Annie have suffered a few bumps along the way, but it doesn't look like it. They have committed their lives to the Lord and he has blessed them financially in their traveling and singing ministry. Yet they are very humble people; they have tasted some of the good things in life, but they're generous and continue to seek God's will for his direction.

After lunch Steve treated us to a new song he'd written, "The Silver Bridge," a ballad about a December 15, 1967, disaster in which a bridge of that name overloaded and overturned, killing forty-four people. Everybody in Steve's home county had someone who either was killed or who nearly missed being on the bridge at the time of its collapse. Christmas that year was a very somber time, and Steve remembers gift-wrapped presents drifting down the river in honor of the dead who would never open them. He did a demo of the song and sent it to his dad, who took it to a local radio station. The station aired the song and it quickly climbed to No. 1 in that county.

"The Silver Bridge" is one of a dozen ballads to be included on an album Steve just wrapped up. Although it's unlike the other albums he and Annie have cut in that it's not explicitly Christian, the songs do carry strong messages that both entertain and prompt serious reflection. The album won't be available in stores but will be sold exclusively at concerts, so if you're interested in getting a copy, I suggest you find out where Steve and Annie will be singing and make yourself part of the audience. You won't be disappointed. Later that evening we sent Ted and Steve ahead to look for a motel, and while they were gone Brian and I had dinner at our first fast-food restaurant of the trip.

As we stood in line to place our order, we struck up a conversation with an older gentleman, his son-in-law, and grandson, who were ahead of us in line. They saw our clothes and asked what we were doing, so we briefly described our trip and how far we had yet to go. We placed our order and when we went to pay, the cashier informed us that our bill already had been taken care of. "The gentleman in front of you paid for everything," she said. And once more we were flabbergasted at the generosity of strangers interested in a couple of soggy cyclists traveling across the country.

After getting our food we sat at a table across from this gentleman and his family and continued to talk. We learned his son-in-law had been an area director for the Navigators, a Christian discipleship ministry, in Tennessee. It turned out the father, son-in-law, and grandson are all Christians. I was struck by their willingness to spend a few dollars on us and make our day a little easier after we'd ridden for such a long time in such sloppy conditions. It's little philanthropies like this which often leave the most lasting impressions and which give us a positive feeling about people. Such small kindnesses may not cost much, but they can change our whole attitude and lift us up and brighten our spirits and make us think,

Maybe things aren't as bad as I thought they were. There are still a few good folks left out there!

It may not be often that we're privileged to observe good theology at work in a fast-food joint, but on that cold, wet night in Gallatin, Tennessee, Brian and I saw it up close and personal. And what we experienced warmed us up right down to our toes.

The next morning we stopped for breakfast in Hartsville at Dillehay's Cafe. It looked to be the only restaurant in town and offered a menu consisting of three selections, posted on an illuminated board above the cash register at the back of the cafe:

> 2 eggs and sausage (or bacon): $2.95
> 1 egg and sausage (or bacon): $1.95
> Sausage and biscuit: $.95

Except they were out of biscuits; white bread or toast would have to do. Orange juice? No. Apple juice? Nope. If you didn't want coffee, tea, or water, you were out of luck. When I asked for *three* eggs instead of two, our waitress's circuits momentarily overloaded and she excused herself to find out from the cook if the request could be honored. (It could be.)

A few men sitting at a table toward the back of the restaurant were eating and needling each other, often in crude terms. We learned it was their custom to gather every Friday at the same spot for breakfast. They saw Brian and me in our bike garb and started asking questions about what we were doing and why. "You doin' it just for the hell of it?" one of the men asked. I briefly explained the reasons behind our trip and casually mentioned that I worked with a "ministry."

Suddenly, the man's whole demeanor changed. He got up from his table and walked over to ours, grabbed a chair and sat down. Gone were the "hells" and "damns" that had punctuated his earlier conversation. In quick succession we learned that he "got saved" in 1977 and that the Good Lord had blessed him ever since. He was frustrated that so many people seemed to live a double life. He was deeply committed to his family and tried in many ways to encourage his children. He believed in being a good Christian and was heavily involved in both his church and his community. We had a good talk, and I really do think our friend is a good guy. But I also think the Good Lord blessed him that morning with a guilty conscience.

It's so easy for most of us to be one person with one group of folks and a completely different person with another group. There's probably a little chameleon in all of us. We want to fit in, we don't want to be excluded, so we change our behavior and language a little (sometimes a lot) to match that of the people we want to impress.

And some of that isn't wrong. The apostle Paul said, "I have become all things to all men so that by all possible means I might save some" (1 Cor. 9:22). When Paul was with Jews, he acted like a Jew. When he was with Gentiles, he acted like a Gentile. When he was with "the weak," he acted like they did. Sounds pretty chameleon-like to me. But *why* did Paul do so much color changing? What was his motivation? I think that's the key to telling the difference between a righteous chameleon and an oily weasel.

Consider again what the apostle said: "I have become all things to all men *so that by all possible means I might save some.*" His goal was not merely to fit in or to be accepted, but to smooth the way for people who didn't know Jesus to be introduced to him. And in the very next verse Paul expands his motivation for righteous chameleonism: "I do all this for the sake of the gospel, that I may share in its blessings." While his primary motivation was evangelism, he also recognized that God had promised to reward faithful service. And he wanted that reward!

I find I must preach this sermon to myself. For most of us, the desire for acceptance is so strong and the fear of rejection so great that we forget the Lord's words in Isaiah: "Do not fear the reproach of men or be terrified by their insults.... Who are you that you fear mortal men, the sons of men, who are but grass, that you forget the LORD your Maker, who stretched out the heavens and laid the foundations of the earth?" (51:7, 12–13).

Afoul of the Law

About noon we passed the Chestnut Mound United Methodist Church, formerly the only congregation in the area. About 1,200 people live in Chestnut Mound, 400 in the immediate neighborhood. These days four other churches serve the little community, including a Church of Christ, a Church of Christ of Prophecy, a Pentecostal group, and a Baptist congregation.

We learned all this from James L. Fletcher, SMSGT, USAF (retired), whose grandfather built the Methodist church from logs on his property. James returned home to this place to retire after being away for forty-six years. He's now the caretaker of the facility and is in the process of mapping the cemetery in back of the church so he can tell visitors where they might find loved ones who are buried there. The whole complex is located on a ridge off the former Walton's Road.

James was keenly interested to know if on our trip we had seen any other church with a bell tower built directly above the front door. As far as he knew, this building was the only one like it anywhere. He asked us to notify him if we discovered a similar church property, but we never saw another church like it. As far as we know, it really is the only one of its kind.

Later that afternoon we stopped for a break between Gentry and Ensor, across the road from Cole's Country Roads store. A few feet into the woods we discovered an old, abandoned cabin with a small graveyard located twenty yards eastward. Picking our way between overgrown shrubs and other underbrush, we found graves dating from the mid-1800s to 1981. While the cabin has been mostly reclaimed by the encroaching forest, a large part of the cemetery is in a clearing, except for the oldest stones whose dates we couldn't make out. Jos. Elrod was born in 1842, for example, but the date of his death was buried along with him in the ground.

Who lived and loved in that cabin? Why did the family eventually leave? Does anyone other than strangers visit the graveyard today? Had any of the deceased made commitments to Christ (the headstones suggest that at least some had)? If so, will we get to meet them someday? Will we get to hear any of their stories?

A graveyard is a great place for questions, but it emphasizes only one stark fact: We all die. That's one reason why I think it's good to visit a cemetery every once in a while. It's a great reality check.

Our break soon came to an end and we pedaled on. We stopped in Cookeville for lunch and asked a local gas station attendant where we might find an acceptable restaurant. He said everything had migrated to the edge of the interstate a couple of miles south. If we wanted a hot meal, we would have to veer off course.

It's sad to see the lifeblood of so many small communities siphoned toward a sterile off-ramp near the speeding masses. It has the same feel as trading your grandparents' handcrafted oak quarter-cut furniture for extruded chrome and artificial leather. There's functionality, but no charm and warmth.

After lunch we decided to abandon Highway 70 (so much for quaint beauty) for a straighter and smoother Interstate 40—despite the sign that said, "Prohibited: Pedestrians, nonmotorized vehicles. . . ." By day's end we had fallen about thirty miles short of our original goal, Harriman, but when you're biking across the country, you go with the flow. And on June 6 the flow stopped in Crossville.

The next day enroute to Knoxville Brian and I tried to reprise our use of I–40, but half an hour into our ride we passed a state patrolman on the side of the road who was helping a wrecker pull a horse trailer out of a ditch. The officer kindly suggested we get off the interstate and back on Highway 70. So we did.

Wet and windy conditions prompted yet another attempt at drafting, but heavy traffic made it impossible and we abandoned the idea. We made it to Kingston for lunch and there made an unpleasant discovery: while the elevation in Kingston is 750 feet, the top of a hill on our route eight miles away stands at an elevation of 2,500.

Our primary stop in Knoxville was scheduled to be at the Cedar Springs Christian Store, the largest independently owned Christian bookstore in the country. A local radio station had arranged for the visit and did a brief interview with me at the store. A spot had been set up inside where we could talk with interested patrons, share some of our stories, and autograph books. One couple stopped by who worked at a local camp run by Jim Wood, an old friend who used to pastor a church in the Atlanta area. I got to know Jim when Focus on the Family acquired partial ownership of a radio station there. Jim had pastored one of our staff members, and now he heads a camping ministry that reaches out to troubled kids. This couple brought us greetings and a note from Jim. After an hour spent enjoying the warm and friendly greetings of those who came by, we were off on the bikes once more.

The ride into Knoxville had a disappointing feel to it because early on in the planning of our trip we had hoped to participate in the Promise Keepers men's conference scheduled for June 6–7 at Neyland Stadium. The local group hosting the meeting asked us to ride into the stadium on Saturday and circle the grounds, then say a few words to the crowd. Officials from the Promise Keepers organization said there was no place in the program for that, so it didn't happen. We were disappointed, but we understood.

Still, I would love to have ridden into a stadium packed with 30,000 men intent on becoming better husbands and fathers. The conference focused on the theme "The Making of a Godly Man" and opened with former Colorado football coach Bill McCartney speaking on the topic "Purity of Heart: Living Clean Before God." On Saturday pastor Tony Evans of Dallas was scheduled to close with a talk called "A Godly Man: The Hope for Our Times."

Brian accepted the Lord a few years ago at one of the first Promise Keepers events, so it would have been great for us to be part of the action in Knoxville. When he was dating Amy in July 1993, Brian accompanied me to the Promise Keepers' event in Boulder, Colorado. I was helping with some of the broadcast efforts then, so we had seats toward the front. On the first night he responded to a gospel invitation given by Greg Laurie. He went forward with hundreds, perhaps thousands, of other men and was gone for half an hour. When he returned Brian just wept and wept. He sobbed, he shook—it was the most dramatic conversion I've ever witnessed. Here was a guy who had such a difficult time showing his emotion—we never saw him kiss Amy in the three years they dated—and yet when he was confronted with a personal relationship with Jesus Christ, all of the barriers came down and he opened himself up completely. It was a classic example of releasing everything, every fiber of his being, to Christ. And it stuck. Brian is a rock-solid guy.

Since 1990, Promise Keepers events have drawn more than two million men to stadiums across the nation. They also draw an assortment of protesters who say they worry that the PK emphasis on men leading in their homes will lead to violence and abuse of women. About a dozen protesters from the National Organization for Women and the University of Tennessee picketed outside the stadium in Knoxville.

Promise Keepers is without question a national phenomenon and we heard about its influence throughout our cross-country trip. On an overpass in Dexter, Missouri, for example, we met an insurance salesman wearing a PK shirt. In 1992 he attended a PK event in Boulder, Colorado, and had a profoundly life-changing experience. He didn't know what to expect before he went and unknowingly took his wife along—probably the only man there with his spouse. He was supposed to stay in dormitory-style accommodations set up for a dozen guys, but when the scheduled roommates saw this fellow's predicament, they doubled and tripled up elsewhere and let this man and his wife have the room to themselves.

On our way through Kansas we picked up a copy of the *Kansas City Star* and read an editorial about Promise Keepers written on the advent of a conference scheduled to take place at Arrowhead Stadium May 30–31. The previous year about 70,000 men had packed that stadium, and a similar crowd was expected this year. The Rev. Douglas DeCelle was quoted as saying, "It's a calling forth of a kind of heroic existence for men to do something to save the culture."[1]

Those are the kind of stories we heard repeated all across the nation. Over and over again we listened to men who described how important Promise Keepers has been in their lives and in the lives of their churches. PK has permeated the fabric of the church more rapidly than any other ministry in America, and the results speak for themselves.

We rode in the dark that night, only the third time we had done so (our first night ride took place in Arizona on the way into Truxton; the second, on the way to Tuba City). A maintenance job on Brian's bottom bracket that we hoped would take just half an hour ended up costing us several hours, forcing us to abandon plans to ride to Newport, another forty miles away. Still, because we wanted to make it to at least the other side of Knoxville, we rode in pitch-black conditions to the edge of town where the van waited to pick us up. Brian was a little nervous about riding without lights and I wasn't thrilled about it either. You never know when that shadow across the road might turn into a crack the size of the Mariana Trench, breaking your wheel and sending you sprawling toward roadside debris. Fortunately, the traffic wasn't heavy and we rode until almost 9:30 P.M.

Then we drove to Newport, where we had been offered two free rooms at the Holiday Inn. Ordinarily we would have skipped the long drive and found something in Knoxville, but it had been made clear to us that the rooms would be free only if we used them; if we failed to show up for some reason, we'd be charged full price. A strange sort of capitalism, perhaps, but it effectively pushed us to Newport.

Yet now we were faced with a new difficulty. By spending the night in Newport, we had put forty miles between ourselves and our morning point of takeoff. We were already almost half a day behind schedule and we didn't want to get further behind. What could we do?

Our solution may not have been elegant, but it was effective. We decided to have a backwards day.

On Sunday morning we hopped on our bikes and rode *west* from Newport to Knoxville, then loaded the bikes in the van and drove back to Newport, eating lunch in the van, thus redeeming time we would have otherwise spent sitting in a restaurant. In that way we would faithfully ride every inch of road along our planned route, yet save ourselves an hour or so of backtracking. It was one instance where we could have our cake and eat it, too.

Up and Over the Appalachians

Wolf Creek Pass in Colorado was definitely the highest peak we had to climb on our journey across America, but compared to the day-long effort of scaling the Appalachians, the Wolf seemed no worse than a playful cub.

Without question, the ride from Knoxville to Asheville, North Carolina, was the most difficult of our trip. The primary culprit was a nasty headwind that whistled and howled and refused to let up all day. The constant wind in our faces, biting and pushing and laughing at our feeble attempts to challenge it, made for a draining, discouraging struggle. We'd pull up a hill, knowing that eventually we'd crest the top and enjoy a nice ride down—only to find that the wind was blowing even more stiffly on the other side and directly in our faces. In order to maintain any kind of speed on our descent, we'd have to pedal—and pedal hard. Forget about coasting! That was spectacularly frustrating.

Add to that the large, rolling hills of the Appalachians— unlike the mountains of Colorado, which climb straight up and then drop straight down, the Appalachians seem to spread out forever, like the rounded, undulating waves that toss ocean liners about on the high seas—and the incessant traffic noise that creates further fatigue, and you have all the makings of a challenging day of riding. We surmounted the Appalachians more slowly than we did Wolf Creek, often making no better than seven miles per hour. A few times we almost came to a standstill as we stood on our pedals and pushed hard, with frighteningly little result.

When finally our arduous trip over the Appalachians was over and we reached the outskirts of Asheville, we wondered where the city could be. We kept feeling as though we were on the verge of entering Asheville, but it didn't happen and didn't happen and didn't happen.

We finally stopped at a gas station–convenience store for a brief rest. A motorcyclist there asked us what we were doing, and in the course of our conversation we inquired about the road ahead. He first began to answer based upon his motorcycle experience, then realized, *No, I need to think about that differently. I need to process this as if I were on a bicycle.* His answer changed, and instead of describing a scenic trip on winding roads through beautiful country, he said, "Well, you do have a steep hill ahead. It lasts—oh, I don't know—six or seven, maybe eight miles. Then you pass through some little town. . . ." After we heard that, whatever else he said didn't seem to matter much.

When at last we reached the city, we were spent. We ended up on some maniacally busy highway and finally stopped for the day on an overpass looking down on a set of ancient railroad tracks, overgrown with weeds and shrubs and bushes. They seemed out of place at that spot in the midst of a busy city and a well-traveled highway and instantly took me back in time. I could almost imagine an old steam engine, a century before, huffing and puffing and pulling cars filled with passengers on its way out of town, heading over the rugged Appalachians.

That night we had dinner with two staff members of WMIT, an Asheville radio station owned by the Billy Graham Evangelistic Association. It's one of the best stations in the country, earning the 1997 Station of the Year award from *Focus on the Family*. The station unexpectedly provided accommodations for us in a local hotel and our hosts led the way there in their car—yet another example of the unforeseen kindnesses that made our journey so richly rewarding.

Because of our late arrival the night before, we didn't get on the road for Day 29 of our adventure until late morning. We wound our way through Asheville, taking a tunnel carved through a mountain in the center of town. My uncle remembered that same tunnel. I suppose there are only a few parts of a cross-country biking adventure that stick in one's mind forever, and cycling through a busy tunnel is certainly one of them. It doesn't leave you feeling especially safe.

Just outside of town we learned a little more about the history of the area. Daniel Boone lived in this region and killed a bear not far from here. Davey Crockett also traveled through the area. In the late nineteenth century, the railroad brought tourists and commerce to town, setting in motion an economic boom that lasted fifty years. In 1895 George Vanderbilt completed Biltmore House, a 250-room mansion situated on 8,000 acres—still the largest private home in America.

Today, Billy and Ruth Graham live just a few miles down the road in Montreat. The Billy Graham Training Center at the Cove—whose purpose is "Training people in God's Word to win others to Christ"—is located on 1,500 acres in the Blue Ridge Mountains just outside Asheville. Billy's influence is substantial throughout the world but nowhere more so than in and around Asheville. In fact, the great evangelist's name looms so large in modern history that Interstate 240 in Asheville has been named "Billy Graham Freeway."

Just before 10:30 a.m. we had pedaled thirteen miles out of town to reach radio station WMIT. It's an interesting facility, a setup that takes you back in time. The station still has the big studios once used for live broadcasts; now they sit empty, live programming having been largely replaced by taped broadcasts and music, CDs and satellite delivery. Through all the change in radio, however, WMIT has beamed incredible hope throughout the area. People living within a radius of perhaps two hundred miles are familiar with WMIT and have been blessed by its programming.

The station began when Billy Graham decided he wanted a strong facility in his own backyard so he could listen to Christian programs. For many years Edna Edwards has been the station's general manager. In the beginning she was a secretary and over time worked her way up to her present position. Edna is highly respected in the industry and is considered a leader for women in management.

After an hour we said good-bye to the staff and pulled out of the station, heading a few miles down the road to Ridgecrest, a beautiful Southern Baptist Conference Center. The business manager there, David Workman, had learned about our trip and wanted to ride a few miles with us.

As we pulled into Ridgecrest's entrance, a light rain began. Now, the *last* thing we wanted to do was to stop and then start again in the rain. Hoping the skies would clear up, we stayed for lunch. After finishing our meal we tuned in to The Weather Channel and soon admitted that it probably was going to rain the rest of the day. So after biking just twenty-two miles—our shortest day of the trip—we decided to call it quits.

Truth be told, it wasn't only the rain that convinced us to throw in the towel so early on Day 29 of our adventure. We needed a break. We were in desperate need of additional rest, of laundry facilities, and of a few hours to work on the bikes. It had been more than ten days since we'd last done a thorough cleaning job, and our bikes, fine machines that they are, weren't designed to tolerate much neglect. I didn't like losing more than six hours of riding, but the amenities of Ridgecrest beckoned and I gladly succumbed to their allure. We found sweet rest at Ridgecrest.

The conference center sits on about 2,200 acres of land in the heart of the Blue Ridge Mountains. Twenty-four buildings totaling more than 52,000 square feet of conference space can house more than 2,500 people at a time, and three auditoriums have a combined seating of about 3,550. The main building features six massive brick and marble pillars standing guard over twenty rocking chairs on the veranda. It's a beautiful complex, the sister of Glorietta Conference Center outside of Santa Fe, New Mexico.

Ridgecrest began in 1907 as the dream come true of Dr. B. W. Spilman, who dubbed the place "the Mountain of Faith." On his first visit to the site—then a wilderness area with a few deserted cabins, a railroad track, and a dirt trail leading west—Spilman knew he had found his Mountain. In 1941 he recalled that first fateful visit:

> Marvelous view! We strolled west leaving the railroad track and came to a spot where Pritchell Hall, the large assembly hotel, is now located. We found a small stream and followed it to its source (now Johnson Spring). Then we climbed the hill west and found an old fence of rotten rails. It was already broken in places. All the party climbed over. I, as usual weighing 260 pounds, came last. I climbed the fence. When I was well balanced on top of the fence, every rail except the bottom one broke. It was a fairly good show.[2]

Today Ridgecrest is a year-round, full-service conference center that attracts up to 70,000 guests annually. A good case can be made (and it has often been claimed) that more commitments to Christian service have been made at Ridgecrest than anywhere else on earth.

Even with the extra, unplanned rest, Brian and I were tired. So it was heaven-sent that for the last four days of our journey we would be joined by two experienced cyclists, Marilyn Wells and Kim Morrow.

Kim drove to Ridgecrest from Greenville, South Carolina, and brought with her not only tremendous biking expertise but oodles of energy. Kim was a member of the International Christian Cycling Club's "Wheels of Thunder" biking team and boasts an illustrious history on the bicycle-racing circuit. A three-time national champion, she would help Brian and me shake off our fatigue and cruise into Virginia Beach with renewed enthusiasm.

While Brian and I enjoyed the day at Ridgecrest, Ted and Steve drove up to Greensboro to pick up Marilyn at the airport. She flew in that afternoon and later that night we all got together for dinner and to strategize our final push to the ocean.

The enthusiasm and energy these two women brought to our adventure saved our lives. Brian and I had not collapsed physically, but mentally we were beginning to wilt under the relentless, day-to-day grind.

A friend of mine, Cynthia Tobias, has been a guest on the broadcast a number of times and is a popular speaker and author. She asked me once if I was familiar with the tracking traits of beagles. Did I know why the dog was so admired for its ability to track animals or humans? No, I had to admit that I didn't. "If you give the scent of your prey, whatever it might be, to a beagle," she said, "that dog will put its head down and pursue that scent tenaciously. When it finally finds the person or the animal, or reaches the point where the scent has disappeared, the dog will lift its head up and be completely disoriented. It's been so consumed with the process, with the course it needed to pursue, that it hasn't paid any attention to its surroundings. It has no idea where it is."

Emotionally, I think Brian and I had reached that point in the ride. We were so consumed with the end, just days away, that we had ceased to notice our surroundings. We were losing our perspective—and Marilyn and Kim helped us regain it.

There were two ways in particular in which Marilyn and Kim put some enthusiasm back into the ride. First, Marilyn is a very frugal person; she can squeeze a nickel out of a penny. For every mile of the next four days she would look for money lying on the road and would find pennies, nickels, dimes, even quarters. So each of us started doing the same thing. It became a game.

Second, since their competitive days Kim and Marilyn had a long history of picking out signs to which they would race, especially city limits signs. Points would be awarded for being the first or second rider to the sign. So while we rode along and talked, we each would have our eyes peeled on the horizon, looking for that sign. Even though you couldn't read it from a distance, you guessed that it might be a city limits sign. Once you saw such a sign, however, you wouldn't share your information with anyone else—perhaps they *didn't* see it, and you could get there first. But even if they *had* seen it, they weren't going to say anything either because they wanted the points, too. So we would jockey for position, continuing our conversation but not really plugged into it because our number-one goal was to be at the right spot at the right moment and in the right gear to make our break for the imaginary finish line. And that was fun, too, a fresh ingredient that livened us up.

Of course, Kim and Marilyn are better riders than Brian and I and they were able to sprint much better than we could—both of them have distinguished themselves as superb sprinters, especially Marilyn. But occasionally Brian or I (OK, more often it was Brian) would succeed in being the first to a city sign.

The real goal, however, was the salt water lapping the shore at Virginia Beach, Virginia. And that goal was getting tantalizingly close.

On June 10, five of us—Marilyn, Kim, David Workman, Brian, and I—took off from Ridgecrest on a magnificent sunny day. Our route took us over Old Highway 70, which had been closed to vehicular traffic a few years after the completion of Interstate 40. Rain has undermined the road in several places. After 70 fell into disrepair, it was decided the road should be closed rather than spend money to fix it. We had the pavement all to ourselves. We met not a single car or truck on this gorgeous, scenic ride up and over the eastern "continental divide," located a few miles east of Ridgecrest. It was no doubt the prettiest hour-and-a-half-ride of our entire journey. And we would have experienced none of it had we not stayed the previous night in Ridgecrest!

We had lunch in Morganton, took back roads which parallel Interstate 40 into Statesville, and finished the day eight miles outside of Mocksville. It had been a superb day morning and afternoon—temperatures in the low eighties, a few white clouds dotting an otherwise sunny sky, the first one we had seen in a week. Beautiful! And it put me in great spirits for my next interview with Dr. Dobson:

Interview Four

Dobson: Hello, Mike! . . . I understand you're now into your final four days of this pedaling trip.

Trout: I can smell the barn from here and I'm at a full gallop.

Dobson: Somebody told me that you left Marion, North Carolina, and you're heading into Winston-Salem.

Trout: That's right, and we'll push on a little northeast toward Virginia and end up on Thursday, we hope, in Virginia Beach.

Dobson: So tonight you will be in Winston-Salem.

Trout: That's right.

Dobson: What's going on in your life, other than that?

Trout: You know we don't know exactly which day it is sometimes. You just get up in the morning and you get on the bike and you ride along and you meet people and you eat breakfast and you eat lunch and you stop at a hotel or somebody's home and you wash some laundry and you go to bed and then you get up and do it all over again.

Dobson: I do understand you had a scary day toward the end of last week.

Trout: Yes, our scariest day occurred when we pedaled out of Poplar Bluff, Missouri, and we headed toward Kentucky. We had lunch that day in Sikeston, Missouri, and then ended up in Paducah, Kentucky. We were on a road that had no shoulder at all and, as a matter of fact, it dropped off on the side. You've seen roads that are under construction and there's just no shoulder?

Dobson: Yes.

Trout: We were cruising along and it was heavy, heavy traffic. It was a little misty in the morning, so the visibility wasn't as good as it could have been.

And I came about as close to a truck as I ever want to get when it's going sixty-five miles per hour.

Dobson: Oh, that's scary!

Trout: It really was. Brian, my son-in-law, was out ahead and he stopped and I pulled up beside him. He was at a road that crossed the highway and he said, "I've been praying for the last half hour that there would be an alternate route." And right at that moment a man pulled up on this crossroad to the stop sign. I pedaled over and asked him if there was another way to get into Sikeston, Missouri, and he said, "Oh, yeah. See that road just a hundred yards down the way? If you'll go down there and turn left, that will take you right into Sikeston." And I said, "Well, we're going to Lambert's Cafe," and he said, "Oh, it's right on that road. That's the most direct route." And so we had an answer to prayer right there in the middle of the highway.

Dobson: A lot of people are praying for you and Brian, Mike. They call here, they're very interested in the trip. They want to know where you are. They want to know who Brian is and what we can tell them about him. People continue to come out and greet you, don't they?

Trout: They sure do. We had a couple just a few days ago who pulled us off to the side of the road. The two of them plus their young daughter were standing behind their car, and they motioned us over and we stopped. They had taken the day off from work—he's a certified public accountant—and they just came out to look for us. They drove a hundred miles to do that. Another couple drove down from Ohio, over three hundred miles, just to spend an evening with us and have some dinner.

Dobson: You're kidding!

Trout: Every time we go into a town there's a gathering. We had a tent the other night outside of a radio station. Time and time again I am so surprised. We have met some wonderful folks. Everybody says, "Tell Dr. Dobson 'hello.'"

There are marvelous stories about how *Focus on the Family* has impacted their lives. And they're just thrilled to be able to touch someone who has touched the studio table where we sit.

Dobson: You know what, Mike? That tells you how much you're loved across the country, and for good reason.

Trout: Well, I certainly appreciate the way we've been honored. And people really are doing that when they want to have a picture or they want to say "hi" or they want to hug your neck and so on. That just lifts us up and honors us.

Dobson: Well, we're going to have to get out of here. Thursday you finish up?

Trout: We're going to finish up, we hope, on the twelfth.

Dobson: And what will that last mile be like?

Trout: First off, I hope it's sunny. The weather forecast is a little iffy, but I hope it's sunny. I'm sure I'll be running on absolute, one-hundred percent adrenaline. We'll just go down into the Atlantic Ocean and put that front tire in there, and then if the weather's not freezing cold, we'll probably flop right into the next wave.

Dobson: We'll try to check in with you again, Mike. I'm going to take a couple of days off for a little vacation, but we'll try to get in touch with you between now and then.

Trout: Now, everybody is saying that I need to do this next year, and you need to come along.

Dobson: Oh, that's very funny!

Trout: You're going to have to start working on it.

Dobson: Hey, tell 'em not to count on that. I'm on a treadmill. I walk just about as far as you ride.

Trout: I know you do.

Dobson: Hey, bless you, Mike. It's always good to talk to you, and we sure miss you.

Trout: I look forward to being back.

That evening we were invited to a potluck dinner at Reynolda Presbyterian Church in Winston-Salem just a block or so from Wake Forest University. As had been the case so often, we were short on time and had to hustle to make the dinner on schedule. Unfortunately, we got lost looking for the church and arrived nearly an hour late. We were concerned that no one would be there when we finally arrived.

We needn't have worried. As we turned the corner and drove into the parking lot, we saw a crowd of perhaps 200 people waiting patiently for us. We parked the van and immediately several folks circled the vehicle. I asked if they were waiting for *Focus on the Family* and the bike riders, and they said yes, they were. It turned out we weren't as late as we had thought; not only did we have incorrect directions, we also had the time of the event wrong. So it all worked together for good, to put things in a biblical vernacular.

Several voices in the crowd shouted, "Oh, we hoped you would ride in on the bike!" So I retrieved my bike from the back of the van, hopped on it, circled around the crowd in the parking lot and then parked in the center of a circle of humanity. Everybody wanted to see the bike and touch it and ask questions about it. There was a mystique about this lightweight conveyance that I had been riding all the way across the country. Time and time again, people just couldn't believe that we had gone as far as we had with those tiny little pedals, those narrow tires, and that seat . . . which to most looked like an instrument of torture.

For half an hour I spoke to the crowd ringing me, standing in the parking lot until it began to get dark. I answered questions and told stories until everyone went downstairs for dinner. Yet even then I didn't get to eat right away. Inside were scores of people who had not come outside. I spoke for another half hour in a meeting room packed to the gills, then answered more questions.

We had a great time at Reynolda Presbyterian Church, but once again got to bed late. Wally Decker of WBFJ-AM radio had put the evening together and also put us up for the night in the Raddison Adam's Mark Hotel downtown. We were more than ready to hit the sack by the time the van pulled into its driveway. Within minutes it was lights out . . . and just three more days to go!

Salt Water in the Air!

Winston-Salem is home to one of the more intriguing examples of the religious heritage of this country. Just a short walk from the city's downtown is Old Salem, a "living history town" that remains largely as it was when it was founded in 1766 as a Moravian congregation village and backcountry trading center. Now one of America's most authentic and well-documented colonial sites, costumed interpreters roam the cobbled streets and re-create household activities and trades common to the late eighteenth and early nineteenth centuries. Homes, outbuildings, trades shops, swept yards, kitchen gardens, and orchards are all carefully preserved to appear just as they did two centuries ago.

And just who were the Moravians? The Moravian Church traces its beginnings to the fifteenth-century martyr John Hus, who was burned at the stake for failing to recant his criticisms of the Roman Catholic Church. After his execution some of his followers formed the *Unitas Fratum,* a church dedicated to a simple life guided by the teachings of Christ. For two centuries the church expanded across Bohemia and Moravia (two regions of the present Czech Republic), but constant persecution caused its numbers to dwindle. Many church members emigrated to safer Germany, where they founded the town of Herrnhut and prospered under the leadership of Count Nikolaus Ludwig von Zinzendorf.

The Moravians were a missionary-sending church with a passion to reach the world for Christ, and from Herrnhut they sent missionaries to America. They established the North Carolina town of Bethabara in 1753 and thirteen years later founded Salem. The church directed both the economic and spiritual affairs of all residents and divided its congregation into groups called "choirs" according to age, sex, and marital status. Music was an important part of life in Salem and "the individual who awoke in the morning to the sound of a trombone choir playing chorales outside the *Gemein Haus* might end his day as part of a chamber orchestra engaged in the performance of works by Mozart or Haydn."[3]

In the mid-nineteenth century Salem ceased to function as a church-owned town, and in 1913 Salem and the newer town of Winston were merged. Yet the influence of early Salem remains and its motto, still emblazoned on crafts sold in gift shops, reminds us of the solid spiritual heritage of this region: "Our Lamb has conquered—Let us follow Him."

Early on the morning of June 11 we clambered into the van to return to the spot outside Mocksville where we had ended the night before. Soon we were on our bikes, headed north to weave our way around Winston-Salem toward the border between North Carolina and Virginia.

The clouds and humidity which dogged the beginning of our ride had burned off by noon. By 6:00 P.M. we had ridden as far as Yanceyville; a little later we ended our day's ride in Roxboro. We were invited to a church in Clarksville, Virginia, for a dessert to be given in our honor after the Wednesday night service, so we got cleaned up, piled into the van, and headed north. A good crowd greeted us, along with a couple of radio stations that wanted interviews.

I was impressed with the congregational mix—as many blacks as whites and even several Asian and Hispanic members, a good picture of what Paul meant in Colossians 3:11 when he said of the church, "Here there is no Greek or Jew, circumcised or uncircumcised, barbarian, Scythian, slave or free, but Christ is all, and is in all." I couldn't help thinking, *My goodness, just a few short years ago you never would have seen that kind of coming together for worship. Blacks had their church in one part of town and whites had their church in another part of town, and never the twain would meet. The separation still exists everywhere, but we're moving in the right direction. Praise God!*

This church was the only one in which an offering was taken for us. Leaders told us, "Use it to help pay your motel bill or your food tomorrow morning." Again, a generous gift gratefully received. What a way to be welcomed into the great state (and the final one) of Virginia!

CHAPTER 8

Home Is Where the Ocean Is

Our penultimate day on the road began June 12 under overcast, humid skies. Before the day was through, it would get both hotter and wetter—but that mattered little, because our goal was in plain sight.

Before noon we four bikers raced to the Virginia border at a little town called Virgilina (although the "official" sign posted by the state inaccurately called it "Virgilinia"). I won the sprint to the city limits sign while Marilyn finished last (Kim cheated and had to be disqualified).

On the edge of town we encountered an enthusiastic welcoming party. In front of a large one-hundred-year-old home, a dozen or so small children and their moms were gathered on the lawn, holding up banners expressing their love of "Adventures In Odyssey" (a *Focus on the Family* drama series for kids) and wishing us safety and success on the rest of our trip. It almost brought tears to our eyes to see these little kids. They had been waiting for some time and they stood motionless as we approached, careful to let us read the various messages printed on their signs. I took all these banners home with me as a memento of the trip.

Wet Enough for You?

High humidity is tough for humans to tolerate; we just don't like all that sticky moisture in the air. But did you know there comes a time when even the air can't take the humidity? That's when it rains.

We learned more about that process early that afternoon. By 1:00 P.M. it was raining; twenty minutes later it was raining more heavily; and ten minutes after that we found ourselves in the hardest rain of our trip. The skies grew black, lightning crackled everywhere, water poured down in torrents, and Brian and I could barely see ahead of us. The traffic behind us, all with lights on, didn't want to scoot around us in such wet and dangerous conditions, and soon a line of cars stacked up half a mile long behind us.

In a few minutes we saw the flashing blue lights of a Virginia State Patrol car and an officer inside pulled Brian and me off to the side of the road. He cracked his window open just a hair to avoid getting soaked himself, and said through the tiny opening, "Fellas, you'll have to pull over. You're slowing traffic."

And I thought, *There's no shelter here! I'm not going to stand in the rain and let all these cars go by and just wait for the rain to stop.* It was a warm spring rain and not particularly cold, but it *was* coming down in buckets, so I replied, "Sir, with all due respect, I don't think we're the problem. We don't have any difficulty with cars going on around us; we'll just hug the side of the road and continue to pedal. I'd rather be *riding* in this rain than *standing* in it."

The officer fumbled a bit with his response and finally said, "Well, I'm just concerned about your safety."

"I appreciate that," I replied, "but we would much prefer to continue to ride. Would you please instruct the cars that have been hesitant to move around us to please go ahead and pass us?"

By then, of course, most of the cars in question already had sped by. Brian and I got back on the road and the officer gave us one last instruction: "Be careful! There's a gas station with an overhang up ahead about two miles and you can pull in out of the weather there." We thanked him and agreed to look for the station, but by the time we arrived at the shelter, the hard rain had stopped and all the cars had vanished into the distance. Our second brush with the law was over.

At Brian's Steak House & Grill we were officially reunited with our families, who had flown into Washington, D.C., with a couple of dear friends the day before. They had driven down to meet us, and our entourage more than tripled in just moments. Joining us for the rest of the trip were Ted's wife, Charlotte; my wife, Nancy; Meredith, our sixteen-year-old daughter; Amy, Brian's wife (and another one of our daughters); Brian's mom, dad, and his brother, J. T.; and Lee and Nicki Bolin, longtime friends and former neighbors from Southern California who moved to Colorado Springs and now are neighbors there. All of them made the long trek to Virginia to witness for themselves the end of our crazy adventure.

It's odd, but I don't recall what we did that evening. I don't know what I ate and I don't remember where I went, if anywhere. But I suppose that shouldn't be too surprising.

Brian and I had been pumping our legs for thirty-two days over a route covering almost 3,200 miles. On this evening we were only a matter of a few miles and a few hours from our goal—the Atlantic Ocean. We found it hard to refrain from salivating over the prospect that the next day we were going to end this long trip. Although I didn't get *really* excited until we got out on the bikes the next day and started pedaling, the night before was still pretty special. In some ways, the anticipation is almost as delicious as the final victory.

But not quite.

Water Never Looked So Good

June 13, Day 33 of our journey. This is it!

What we were about to do we had done before, but today was different. I had the same feeling I suppose a player in the Super bowl might have. We were about to do what we had been doing for four weeks, but these would be the final pedal strokes. I didn't expect to get emotional, but raw emotions surged through me. Success was in the air!

I had also learned something about myself: I was capable of far more emotionally and physically than I had ever imagined. Within obvious limitations, I felt as if a new world had opened up. I could accomplish what before had seemed unthinkable. The wall which we all erect around ourselves, the barrier that defines our limits, had a door in it! And the world on the other side looked bigger than the one I'd been living in all these years. It was an intoxicating morning!

We got started shortly after 8:00 A.M. The muggy air made everything seem damp, but what did it matter? The weather-man forecast a chance of showers and a high temperature of eighty-seven degrees, but who cared? Everyone on the trip was eager for it to be done. No euphoria yet—more like grim deter-mination—but a light spirit pervaded the day. The Atlantic beckoned, and we were anxious to answer its call.

Brian's brother, J. T., wanted to get a feel for the sensation of cross-country biking, so he joined us on the road for about an hour, using the spare mountain bike we kept in the van. An hour before noon we stopped at a Burger King for an early lunch, where J. T.'s mini-adventure ended and we fueled up for the final push to the ocean. Also at the Burger King we finally met face-to-face with a video crew from the Christian Broad-casting Network. CBN and my publisher, Zondervan, had been discussing the possibility of capturing part of our trip on video. Partway into the adventure an agreement was struck that we end our adventure in Virginia Beach, Virginia, the home of CBN, rather than in Myrtle Beach, South Carolina, my origi-nally planned stopping point.

I had chosen Myrtle Beach for two reasons. First, the route from Santa Monica, California, to Myrtle Beach is one of the shortest routes available from the Pacific to the Atlantic, almost 250 miles less than a course ending in Virginia Beach. Second and perhaps most important, Myrtle Beach was the city where my uncle ended his own trip in 1995. And therein lies a story of its own.

On June 5, 1995—Day 43 of his trip—Tom Gilfoy was perched on the cusp of a great personal triumph.

At sixty-three years of age, he had pedaled 2,880.9 miles on a solo trip across America and needed to cover only sev-enty more miles to finish his remarkable journey. "I marveled over this being my last day," he wrote in his journal. "I didn't think it would ever get here, but if all went well, sometime about mid-afternoon I expected to ride right into the ocean. I planned to jump off my bike and take a head-first dive into the first wave."

Most sentences have key words or phrases, and the two sentences above are no exception. The key phrase in Tom's first sentence is "if all went well," while the key words in the second are "I planned."

Unfortunately for Tom, all did not go well as planned.

About sixteen miles from the beach, something happened. But I'll let Tom tell the story himself:

> I eventually reached Conway as Highway 501 skirts that city's southerly edge. When I approached a shopping center parking lot, there was a car sitting at an exit waiting for a break in southbound traffic to pull out onto the highway. The driver must have been looking for the break over his left shoulder, as he obviously didn't see me as I started to ride by, directly in front of him. Suddenly he lurched forward. I yelled, but it was too late and he hit me broadside. The impact sent me sprawling out onto the highway.
>
> The next thing I knew, I was lying flat on my back in the middle of Highway 501 with the rain hitting me in the face. I instinctively knew I shouldn't move, and I'm not sure I could have even if I'd wanted to. An older gentleman came over and started apologizing. He said he was sorry but he hadn't seen me. He said, "Why don't you jump in with me, and I'll take you over to the hospital." I replied, "No, thanks. I think I'll wait for the ambulance."
>
> Things get a little blurry in my memory about here, but I do remember that a pretty good-sized crowd started to build and that as I looked up, there must have been seven or eight people holding umbrellas over me. I thought, *This is the end of "Lonely Are the Brave," I'm Kirk Douglas, and a truck just knocked me off my horse.* The only problem with the comparison was that no one shot my bike as they had Kirk's horse.

At the hospital Tom learned that he had broken his right collarbone, but doctors thought it would be OK for him to ride the last few miles of his trip to the ocean, whenever he felt up to it. He took the next day off and planned on finishing his adventure the day after that. But he wasn't prepared for the way it ended.

Newspaper reporter Laura Lewis from the *Myrtle Beach Sun News* heard about Tom's accident and briefly interviewed him and his wife Dody the day of the mishap. The next morning the Gilfoys were both surprised to see Tom had made the front page. That press coverage then began an avalanche of other events.

- Lou Finkle, a member of a local bicycle-riding club, called Tom at his hotel to inquire whether he'd like a riding escort to finish his ride. Tom said sure—and wound up with about a dozen fellow cyclists the next day.
- A bicycle shop called with an offer to fix Tom's damaged bike. Tom accepted, then learned that the owners would be among those riding with him the next day and that they wanted to box up his bike and ship it home to California when he was through riding, thus sparing him the effort and expense.
- The police chief from the city of Conway insisted on providing Tom with a police escort. The men in blue from Conway were joined by law enforcement representatives from the state highway patrol, the county of Horry, and the city of Myrtle Beach.
- Four local television stations lined up to cover the final ride on Wednesday, while a local disc jockey planned to broadcast live from his radio truck.
- The mayor of Conway declared June 7, 1995, "Tom Gilfoy Day," made a speech to recognize Tom's accomplishment, and presented him with a key to the city.
- Carol Liu, the mayor of Tom's own city of La Cañada Flintridge, proclaimed June 21, 1995, "Tom Gilfoy Day" and said that by his feat he had "brought tremendous honor and prestige to the City of La Cañada Flintridge."

On June 7 Tom finally reached his goal, later writing that:

> The waiting crowd surged forward and began applauding as we hit the beach. If I wasn't overwhelmed before, I sure was now. I'm sure the disc jockey reporting live contributed to the size of the crowd, but I also think that there was something else at work peculiar to this part of the country—a showing of good, old-fashioned, Southern hospitality.
>
> When I pushed my bike out into the surf with flash bulbs popping and TV cameras whirring away, a cheer went up. I gave my bike to a policeman to hold and turned

around and dove into the next wave. I still had my helmet, bike shoes and watch on, and my wallet was still in my pocket. I didn't care. The disc jockey came into the surf after me for an interview.

Soon all the bikini-clad high school and college-age girls were coming up and asking to have their pictures taken with me. No problem. I accommodated them all....

For a moment or two, I was left standing in the waves by myself while a half circle of people stood staring at me. *What am I supposed to do now?* I thought. I didn't know, so I gave a little impromptu speech, the essence of which was that you, too, can have this happen to you if you hire someone in a car to run you down when you're about to finish a cross-country bicycle ride. However, I advised against hiring the same person I had, as he got too carried away with his assignment and hit me too hard. The kids ate it up and, before I knew it, one of the TV announcers was in the water, egging me on....

Our own day in the sun would not come in Myrtle Beach and would not (we hoped) be attended with police escorts and mayors' proclamations prompted by broken bones, but would rather occur many miles to the north in Virginia Beach.

Kendall Kempf, a producer with CBN, met us about twenty miles from the beach and gave us ten photocopied maps showing the best way to reach the sand. He and his camera crew would shadow us throughout that final route, taking video of the ride from several vantage points. It was at this moment that my adrenaline really started to flow. *We're really going to make it!*

The only other time I could recall a rush like this was when our second child was born. Our first daughter, Rebekah, was a breach baby and I wasn't allowed in the delivery room. But Amy was positioned normally and the doctor gave his OK for me to be there for her arrival. Any dad who has watched that little life peek out for the first time knows the feeling I'm trying to describe. "Honey, we did it! *You* did it! He did it!" Wow. You want to cry and laugh at the same time. And eventually you just stand there with a silly, Cheshire Cat grin covering your giddy face. That's close to how I felt as the coastal sands of Virginia Beach crept ever nearer.

At 12:30 P.M. we suffered one last flat tire; the honor went to Marilyn. The repair took a little longer than expected because the tire pump I normally carried on my bike had vanished. I still can't figure out where it went. Surely I or one of the other three cyclists would have noticed had it fallen off; but it was nowhere to be found. We never did find it. I guess we were all so distracted by the imminent end of our journey that we simply didn't notice when it went AWOL.

But not even flat tires or a missing bicycle pump could stop the excitement now. Once the adrenaline began to pump for me, I got more and more excited and found myself out ahead of the group (when normally I was at the other end).

When finally we turned onto General Booth Boulevard, the road leading straight to the beach, my "beagle" instincts had risen to full strength—my nose pointed toward the sand and I didn't notice much else. Later I heard that in turning from Dam Neck Road onto General Booth, I didn't quite make the green turn arrow and almost got hit. But there was to be no police escort for me.

No police escort, that's true, but we did pick up a bicycle escort from two uniformed security guards sent by CBN. They asked us to follow them as they led the way to the beach.

By now we could hardly contain our excitement—we could smell the salt air, hear the waves crashing against the shore, see the sun glinting off the Atlantic's vast blue surface. But this is television, folks, and you don't get by with one take.

The CBN film crew wanted to make sure it got just the right shots for its video, so even though we were within a few hundred yards of the ocean, we were asked to take a few detours through downtown. We could see the finish line, we could smell the barn, if you will—and then we spent another forty-five minutes turning this corner and riding down that street and waiting at this stoplight to satisfy the video folks. Although I know it was necessary and I appreciate the great job Kendall and his crew did, I'll admit it got a little frustrating.

At 3:10 P.M., just over 843 hours of pedaling after pulling away from the Pacific ocean I stepped off the dry sand and dipped my bicycle's front tire in the Atlantic.

I was surprised at the emotions that flooded over me. For several moments I found it difficult to speak. I'm generally not real emotional, but a flood of feelings overwhelmed me. It was almost impossible to believe that Brian and I had started out thirty-five days before in Santa Monica, California, and had ridden every inch of the 3,150 miles to Virginia Beach, Virginia. Had we cheated or skimped at all, I know the emotion I felt at that moment would have eluded me. But we hadn't cheated. We hadn't skimped. We hadn't cut one corner or skipped one mile. *We had ridden our bikes all the way from one coast to the other!* What a marvelous feeling of accomplishment!

And then it was time for the interviews. First I placed a call to Dr. Dobson.

Final Interview

Dobson: I just got a note on my desk and I came running down here to the studio. It said that you were only five minutes away from the beach. Is that right?

Trout: It came quicker than I thought. Yes, we're right in Virginia Beach. We're going to turn the corner here up at a stoplight and try to find ourselves a way down to the sand.

Dobson: What an exciting moment! Are you emotional?

Trout: Well, I have been all the way in. It's . . . it is! *It is!*

Dobson: I'll bet! After three thousand miles, I just can't believe it.

Trout: It's hard to imagine. You think back over all that you've done, and it's almost like living a mini-lifetime. Because you've traveled so many miles and you started from one point and ended as far as you can go in the other direction. You almost want somebody to say, "Well done, good and faithful servant."

Dobson: Hey, there are a million people saying it to you right now, Mike.

Trout: It's been a good day. The Lord gave us some good weather, a great tailwind today. We just cruised. The sun is shining, it's a perfect time in the afternoon. Our families came in last night, so it just couldn't be a nicer conclusion to a very, very long trek. And I look forward to talking with you about it in much greater detail and sharing some of the fun stories.

Dobson: Can you see the beach from where you are right now?

Trout: I sure can! I sure can!

Dobson: Do I understand the 700 Club came out and videotaped you?

Trout: They have been with us all day long and they're going to be down at the ocean when we get there. That should be in just a matter of minutes.

Dobson: Are there any other people who have kind of cheered you along on this last leg?

Trout: Oh, definitely! We had folks all along the way today, cars honking and people stopping us. But we've had our heads down today—you know, that old phrase "You can smell the barn." We could smell the salt water and we knew this was the end of it. But it's almost hard to imagine that we've done all of this. I think back over each and every day and the experiences that we've had. This is something that I'll remember for the rest of my life and talk about, and I think I probably made some friends that I'll stay in touch with for the rest of my life. It's just been a marvelous, marvelous time.

Dobson: Now that it's within seconds of being over, Mike, do you wish that it would continue or are you glad to have it done?

Trout: No, I really look forward to getting back into the studio with you, to be honest.

Dobson: Well, we've really missed you, Mike, and I'm anxious to talk to you about more of the details.

Trout: Yes. I'll be back next week and we can talk more about it.

Dobson: Okay, Michael. Hey, it's an exciting moment and *I'll* say it to you: "Well done, my friend!"

Trout: Thank you! I can't wait to tell you about all the folks who've said to say "hi" and give you a hug on your neck. It's just been a great time.

Dobson: Come on home, Mike.
Trout: All right. I'll show you the slides.

Moments later CBN interviewed me on the beach, with about thirty-five people standing nearby. As I waded into the ocean with the surf crashing around me, the cell phone rang and on the line was Dick Bott. I had spoken live with Dick over his network of stations every morning for the last three weeks, and this would be our final conversation.

> **Bott:** This is Dick Bott. We are live at this moment, and as we promised you yesterday, we are going to talk to Mike Trout at the very conclusion of this trip he has taken on a bicycle from Santa Monica, California, clear to the Atlantic Ocean on the east coast at Virginia Beach, Virginia. Mike, are you there?
> **Trout:** I am here. I'm standing in the water! My shoes are soaked! We made it!
> **Bott:** Mike, how many miles did you have on your bicycle before you got off it and into the water?
> **Trout:** About 3,200 miles. It's been a *long* way since Santa Monica. It's just been a marvelous day. We've had beautiful weather. We had rain, just pouring rain yesterday, and we were freezing cold. Today it warmed up and we had the wind at our back for the first time in weeks, and the sun came out. It couldn't be a nicer close. I'm looking at the beach, at the boats moving along the shore here, and the seagulls—and all kinds of people greeting us!
> **Bott:** When we talked to you yesterday, you said that toward the end of this journey, the miles seemed to get longer and it seemed to be more arduous.
> **Trout:** That's true. However, today went by very quickly. I don't know what it was; I think it was the tailwind. You know, it was almost like the Lord had his hand at our back. And—oh my, I just . . . I'm *real* wet right now. The tide is coming in or something—he just pushed us along, and every time we checked how far we had to go, it was a lot closer than we thought. So it's been a great day and a wonderful trip.

Bott: One other thing. There have been some things in my life that were very, very difficult to look ahead and accomplish. Nothing, however, like what you have just done. Does it make you feel that when the challenge is so great and the motivation is so strong, there's an exhilaration that just can't be imagined?

Trout: There's nothing like perseverance. The Bible talks a lot about persevering when you think you can't finish, when you're sure that the situation is going to be tougher than you can handle. There's great wisdom in that, in pushing on through. The exhilaration of completion is unreal, and it is something that you will not only remember for the rest of your life, but you will remember each time another hill is put before you, another challenge is there, another reason to quit exists. If you just stick with it, He'll help. There are so many lessons to learn on a trip like this. I think I'll be processing it for months and months.

Bott: God bless you. Thank you so much for sharing this portion of your life with us and our listeners.

Trout: Thanks, Dick!

CHAPTER 9

Postscript

As I write this postscript, the words of a poignant tune by the late John Denver are rolling over in my mind: "Hey, it's good to be back home again."

How true that is! While I thoroughly enjoyed my little adventure, I wasn't about to shed any tears that it was over—except for tears of joy that at last I could return home. I've discovered that Dorothy Gale from Kansas was exactly right: There's no place like home.

I'm still riding and watching what I eat. After all that effort, I don't want to go backward healthwise. I have slipped back into the old work routine, with endless meetings, hours in the studio, and a constant stack of paperwork. Old stresses have returned and I'm no longer the master of my own schedule.

As I watch the U.S. flag flutter outside my office window, I find myself drifting back to the high desert of Arizona and a newly deserted U.S. Route 66. With this kind of wind at my back, we might be able to cruise at twenty-eight miles per hour! I can't help but evaluate every road shoulder and envision myself moving with the traffic. I've injected a strange drug into my bloodstream and I can't get rid of it. The euphoria has grabbed me and I'm hooked. Feeling good feels good. My HDL is up and I intend to keep it there. Everyone says, "You look great!" and I like that, too. Why didn't I do this years ago?

So, What Did You Learn?

"Now that your cross-country adventure is over," I've often been asked, "what would you say you've learned from your trip? What have you discovered about the heart of America? And do you have any further adventures in the offing?"

Before I sum up what I learned on my bicycle trip, allow me to recount the conclusions reached by Henry Wigglesworth, a young man who spent sixty-three days in the summer of 1997 bicycling from Baltimore, Maryland, to Portland, Oregon. Wigglesworth teaches legal writing at Seattle University School of Law in Tacoma, Washington, and writes,

> Some cross-country cyclists have told me about the incredible insights they gain during the long hours spent staring at asphalt. One even told me he found God. (He must have had a better map than I.) Although I can't claim to have had any Earth-shattering epiphanies, I can say that the trip changed me forever—and I'm not talking only about the callouses on my rump.

Here are the top . . . lessons that I learned from the road:

- Our country is, by and large, unpopulated. All the politicians who are concerned about immigrants crowding us out of our neighborhoods should pay a visit to Wyoming, where the largest town has 50,000 people and exits off the interstate are dirt. Or South Dakota, where the state's flagship university is located in a town of 5,000 (with the beautiful name of Vermillion). Or Eastern Oregon, which is so unlike the populous western part of the state that it's not even in the same time zone. These are places where cows outnumber people. . . .
- People are nice. As a native New Yorker, I was raised to be suspicious of people who offered me things for free: Question Generosity was our credo. But after the 10th family offered me and my girlfriend Laura a place to stay for the evening and cooked us dinner and breakfast, I stopped thinking of them as potential ax-murderers. Not only did families take us into their homes, but bike mechanics often did not charge us for their labor. Even a trucker, the supposed sworn enemy of bicyclists, saved our lives once by giving us water when we were dying in the middle of nowhere. . . .
- Mayberry, R.F.D., is alive and well. We all remember the town of Mayberry on "The Andy Griffith Show," a place where nobody locked their doors and even the jail

had no key. Well, Mayberry still exists along the back roads of this country. As we rode through town after town, we were constantly surprised to see bicycles, unlocked, on the lawns in front of houses. "Don't these people know any better?" was my first reaction until I realized that I was the one who needed re-education to shed my cynicism.

- Road surfaces are completely random. Before this trip, I thought that highways were designed by some bureaucrat with a Ph.D. in asphaltology, who carefully chose the right surface according to the region's weather and number of vehicles. Now I know that they are randomly built with whatever material is left over after all other public works projects are finished. Sometimes when we entered a new state, the road surface would suddenly go from smooth blacktop to an embedded pebble surface, for no apparent reason. The width, or even existence, of a shoulder also varied. Even interstate highways, which you would think are subject to uniform standards promulgated by an assistant deputy undersecretary of transportation, were fickle in their surface and width.[1]

I concur with all of Wigglesworth's observations; from my perspective he's right on target. But I also reached a few of my own conclusions:

- America really is a "grassroots" nation. When you meet and sit down with the people of Leoti, Kansas; or Paducah, Kentucky; or Tuba City, Arizona; you quickly realize that the opinions and viewpoints broadcast so incessantly from such media centers as New York and Los Angeles are often not broadly accepted (or even welcomed) among the men and women living in the nation's heartland. These people care deeply about their families, about their churches, about their communities. They treat issues of faith seriously and strive to walk humbly with their God. They want their children to grow up in a land where Christ is honored and worshiped and where his name is invoked reverently, not as a term of profanity.

- People are passionately concerned for their families. No doubt most of those who sought us out along our journey did so because they admire the work of *Focus on the Family*, but even when we spoke with people who had never heard of *Focus*, this deep concern for family surfaced time and again. Fathers and mothers want to know what they can do to help their children blossom into productive and godly citizens, and they want to be reassured that such a thing is still possible today. More than ever, I know now that it really *is* possible, for I met scores of young people who are living testaments to the concern and love of their parents. As long as America produces young people like these, it has a future.

- Life can be incalculably sad when it is lived disconnected from the roots of family and faith. I can't get Rodney Jones out of my mind. You'll recall he's the man we met outside of Kingman, Arizona. Aimlessly biking his way across America, Rodney made his living from town to town by picking up pop and beer cans and selling them for scrap. Family life had grown too painful for Rodney, and several months prior to our meeting he had abandoned his family back in the Midwest. Ditching a family may seem like an attractive option when the going gets rough, but Rodney's life shows such an option to be both deceptive and ruinous. A life without hope isn't much of a life at all.

- Most people are incredibly generous and kind. I don't think I'll ever get over the superabundant kindnesses that were lavished upon us throughout our trip. Wherever we went we encountered men and women eager to pay for a meal here or arrange for a night's lodging there. On a post-trip *Focus on the Family* broadcast dedicated to my adventure, I recounted some of these kindnesses to Dr. Dobson and he replied, "I just don't understand the love we get."

Shortly thereafter we received a note from a listener who wrote,

> I wept when you said to Mike, 'I don't understand the love we get.' ... Focus on the Family, by its very

nature, represents everything that we hold near and dear to our hearts. You raise a standard of excellence, truth, integrity, justice, love and hope that is so desperately lacking in our society today.... Twelve years ago I almost divorced my husband and I wrote a letter to Focus. A counselor from Focus on the Family called me and talked to me for over an hour on the phone. That was a powerful influence on my life. My family is still intact today and oh, what I would have missed if I had destroyed my family.... We love you (and Focus on the Family) because you love God with all your heart(s) and because you are obedient to the calling He has given you. It is that simple.

I beg you, don't allow the cynicism of the age to deceive you into thinking kindness has vanished from our land. It hasn't. Take a trip across this great country and see for yourself!

- Prayer is a mighty weapon that connects us personally to the overwhelming power of God. Our trip was remarkably free of injuries, of mishaps, of sickness, and of dangerous wrong turns. Why? I have zero doubt about the correct answer: Faithful people were praying for us. Before the trip I knew that many prayers were being offered on our behalf, but I had little idea of the vast numbers of prayer warriors interceding for us until I returned to my office. Then I read and heard of hundreds of intercessors, just like John Gearhart from Hurst, Texas: "I was inspired by Mike Trout's cross-country ride. Although I live in Texas, I was with him in spirit. I prayed daily for their safety and health. I was excited to hear that the adventure had a very happy ending." Yes, God does hear and he does answer! The safety we enjoyed throughout our adventure is public evidence of that fact.

Anyone for Another Adventure?

One of my hopes as I started out across the United States on my Road Logic bicycle was that I might nudge others to plan an adventure of their own. Since my return I've been

gratified to learn that some folks really have taken up my challenge. Texan Glen Peeples, for example, wrote to say, "Mike,
we are glad you are home from your 3,000-mile bike trip. In the
year 2000 I plan on celebrating my thirty-ninth birthday the
same way. My wife thinks I have lost my mind."

No, he hasn't lost his mind. But he may have found an
adventure! And so may other listeners. One wrote, "I enjoyed
hearing of Mike Trout's recent bike trip. It sort of makes me
wonder if I should, at fifty-seven, try something like this. . . . I
am so often amazed to see how folks can find exciting things to
do, and this is such a counter to those young people who con-
tend 'there is nothing to do.' Perhaps Mike will have some kind
of essay on this adventure, with pix?"

Well, the "essay with pix" is the package you now hold
in your hands. May it inspire many others!

And what of further adventures for me? Colonel William
J. McCullough (retired) wrote of just that possibility: "While
driving home, I listened to the fascinating and emotional
account of Mike's good-will journey across our marvelous
country. After reaching the inside of my garage, I continued
to listen to the closing about the possibility of another adventure. My eyes were filled with tears (remarkable for a former
police captain and army colonel)."

And it may be more than just a "possibility"! Next year I
hope to embark on another cross-country bicycle trip—but this
time, from the south of merry old England to the north of misty
Scotland! A British radio friend of mine wants to follow the
example of Don Hughes (KJIL, Meade, Kansas) and take such
a trip to raise money for his station. He asked me to join him
. . . and I think I will!

You see, getting older doesn't mean you have to stop living. That was proven to me once and for all by a listener who
sent me a story about Hermon K. Hoffer. Hermon started riding his bicycle in 1969 and since then has pedaled 94,831 miles.
He rode across the country twice, first from east to west in 1980
at the age of seventy-five, and the next year from west to east.
He often left behind business cards featuring a black and white
photo of himself on his recumbent bike and the slogan, "Have
bicycle, will travel!" Hermon died June 7, 1997, as a result of an

accident while riding his bike in his hometown of Ashley, Michigan. He was ninety-two years old. [2]

I want to be like Hermon! If I'm still pedaling my way across America at age ninety-two, I'll be the most grateful man on the planet. And I'll also still be thanking Hermon for bringing to my attention a poem by Edgar A. Guest called "Old Age." I think it's wisdom to live by.

> *I used to think that growing old*
> *was reckoned just in years,*
> *But who can name the very date*
> *when weariness appears?*
> *I find no stated time when man*
> *obedient to a law,*
> *Must settle in an easy chair and*
> *from the world withdraw.*
> *Old age is rather curious,*
> *or so it seems to me,*
> *I know old men at forty and*
> *young men at seventy-three.*
> *I'm done with counting life by years*
> *or temples turning gray,*
> *No one is old who wakes with joy*
> *to greet another day.* [3]

Notes

Chapter 1: *Why* Are You Doing This?

1. Jeffrey Zaslow, "Straight Talk," *USA Weekend* (May 23–25, 1997): 15.

Chapter 2: Just 3,149 Miles to Go

1. "Special Resource Study Route 66," United States Department of the Interior, National Park Services, NPS D-4 July 1995, 10.
2. David Darlington, *The Mojave* (New York: Henry Holt, 1996), 18.
3. Ibid.
4. Paul M. Lewis, *Beautiful California Deserts* (Beaverton, Ore.: Beautiful America, 1979), 19.

Chapter 3: Nothing Much But Staggering Beauty

1. "Town named for 'Old Bill' Williams," Visitor's Guide, *Williams: Gateway to the Grand Canyon* (Spring/Summer 1997): 8.
2. William P. Barker, *Who's Who in Church History* (Old Tappan, N.J.: Fleming H. Revell, 1969), 191. McPherson began her ministry as a missionary to China along with her husband Robert Semple. After his death, Aimee returned to the United States and married Harold McPherson, from whom she separated to pursue an itinerant revival-healing ministry. She soon settled in Los Angeles, where for more than twenty years her colorful meetings drew immense crowds. She eventually gained notoriety by a third marriage and subsequent divorce, accompanied by never-proven charges of sexual affairs. She died in 1944 from an overdose of sleeping pills.

Chapter 4: Staring Down the Wolf

1. David Lamb, *Over the Hills*: *A Midlife Escape Across America by Bicycle* (New York: Random Times Books, 1996), 148.
2. To contact Bay and Peggy Forrest at Focus Ministries, use their e-mail address: forrest@pagosasprings.net.

Chapter 5: Drafting Through Kansas

1. Sarah Lunday, "Storm's wrath unites a community," *The Wichita Eagle*, May 27, 1997, 11A.
2. Ibid.

Chapter 6: R & R in the Show Me State

1. "Fun Things You Didn't Know About Missouri," *Missouri Traveler Guide* (February–June 1997): 7.

2. "Little Known and Widely Known Facts About Missouri," *Missouri Traveler Guide* (February–June 1997): 25.

3. Cheryl Russell, "The Baby Boom Turns 50," *American Demographics* (December 1995), as reproduced on American Demographics Marketing Tools home page, 1, 2.

Chapter 7: Where Will You Spend Eternity—Smoking or Nonsmoking?

1. "Promise Keepers Return: Critics and Cheerleaders differ on worth of rally," *The Kansas City Star*, My 28, 1997, cb.

2. "A Mountain of Faith," Ridgecrest Baptist Conference Center brochure.

3. Hunter James, *Old Salem Official Guidebook* (Winston-Salem, N.C.: Old Salem, 1994), 7.

Chapter 9: Postscript

1. Henry Wigglesworth, "Your Voice: Cyclist leaves cynicism behind on road," *The News Tribune* (August 24, 1997).

2. Jennifer Vincent, "94,831 miles of living and loving every mile," *Clinton County News* (June 15, 1997): 1.

3. Edgar A. Guest, "Old Age," *Clinton County News* (June 15, 1997): 1.